WRONG
TO
RIGHT

ISBN: 1-4392-5917-8

EAN13: 9781439259177

WRONG
TO
RIGHT

JOHN PERFETTO

Table of Contents

Dedication

Only one in five businesses will see its fifth-year anniversary. This book is dedicated to the owners of the four businesses that don't make it. Don't stop trying. Success in business follows failure in much the same way that adulthood follows adolescence. There is far less reward in remaining entrepreneurially thirteen your whole life. Hang in there. Timing has a lot to do with the outcome of a rain dance.

Foreword

"The real distinction is between those who adapt their purposes to reality and those who seek to mold reality in the light of their purposes."
—Henry Kissinger

"Reality is that which, when you stop believing in it, doesn't go away."
—Philip Dick

"Humankind cannot stand very much reality."
—T. S. Eliot

The intent of this book is to help the average business owner better understand the long-standing education he has received and the deviation from reality therein. This education, either formally taught at the institutional level or informally taught by our families, friends, and the media, in many ways sets us up for failure—either failure caused by either poorly understood knowledge of how the world actually works or failure caused by a fear of failure and consequent paralysis.

My twenty years of experience in the business world has seen a multitude of positions: engineer, quality control manager, plant manager, project manager, general manager, sales representative, president, business owner, and CEO. My mechanical engineering degree started my career in the world of manufacturing, which progressed from the technical, to management, to sales, and eventually to owning several successful and some unsuccessful business entities. I consider myself a financial success as defined by the United States Small Business Administration, and my income places me in the top one-half of 1 percent in the world.

While I feel qualified to offer my advice to other business owners as someone who has achieved success, I feel I also must warn the reader that I do not consider my advice to be the only approach that will lead to success. The wonderful thing about this country is that it affords everyone—and I do mean everyone—the opportunity to achieve success in the business world. Some may not recognize the opportunity in front of them, but I would offer that if opportunity does not exist for an individual in the United States, it does not exist, period.

My suggestions are certainly not the only way or, for that matter, the absolutely correct way, but they are the proven rantings of this madman and are what I have seen work, and of course, I am a living testament to their potential. This book will not ensure success. Only you possess that power. This book merely offers suggestions to change your mind-set from a worker bee to the queen bee. Our friends, families, and especially the media don't like queen bees. Misery is a solution that does not like dilution and is better served in concentrated form in equal parts among the masses. We have been told to forego the delusional thoughts of breaking free from our bonds of mediocrity and get comfortable on the couch. If you are indeed looking to undo the decades of the "you can't do that" indoctrination, by all means keep reading. If you are looking for a magic formula, please put this book back in the box and return it to Amazon.

Apparently, you have chosen the former. I congratulate you and look forward to sharing our time together. Our journey begins with your brain and its oh-so-very dangerous contents.

Chapter 1

Overcoming Our Education and Misconceptions

I. Business owners clean toilets.

Our heads are poorly prepared for business ownership. Business ownership requires us to make purely logical decisions with one and only one thought in mind: does this decision make money or lose money? This question is easy to understand and equally easy to ask ourselves. How we answer this question is where most of us come off the rails. And like a train wreck in slow motion, it is difficult to watch.

Let's look at a very simple example. In starting a business, most quickly find that the process of cleaning the place of business is one of those little pesky items that is easily overlooked, especially in the budgeting process. I am speaking, of course, of simple housekeeping and the associated costs. A very small office, under one thousand square feet, is easily cleaned with monthly fees of $100 or so in most cities. The time involved in cleaning is thirty minutes per week, or two hours a month. This equates to $50 per hour.

When I questioned a business owner friend of mine, who by the way was brand new to the business world having just hung out his shingle as a money manager, he said it was beneath him to clean his own office. After all, he was degreed as well as state licensed to manage millions of dollars of the public's money. Running a vacuum was hardly worthy of such an individual. Let's ask our question with regard to making or losing money and see how illogical his answer was.

His practice was brand new. His personal income at the time the question was posed was roughly $65,000 per year. This is equivalent to $31.25 per hour. Do you see a problem here? Paying a cleaning service $50 an hour when your top-line income is $31.25 per hour is insane. I don't care how important your sheepskins make you feel; that cleaning service is making more money than you are. When we ask, "Will this make money or lose money?" our answer is what? Sorry, Mister Money Manager, I would like to introduce you to your new best friend, the toilet brush. Stay an extra half-hour each week and do your own cleaning. His decision was losing money.

After expenses were removed, our money manager was netting $20 an hour, and this was before taxes. The $50 an hour he would save in cleaning the office himself was the equivalent of giving himself a $1,200-a-year top-line revenue increase or the net effect of a free telephone line, Internet service, electricity, or some other service he could not provide himself.

Intuitively, no one believes the owner of the business cleans his own toilets. Surprisingly, most do, at least until the business becomes viable and can afford cleaning services. When most Americans see or think of business owners, they are considered after the fact. The "fact" here is what many like to call critical mass. The business has developed enough cash flow and enough clients that the entity is moving on its own. The magic has already occurred, and poof, there is a business. What it took to make that magic happen is just that, magic, because most people either cannot or will not take the time to understand how this magic trick is performed. Business owners only order people around and collect checks. They don't clean toilets. If you go into business with this thought process, you're in for a major shock.

If you're in business with this thought process, you may be out of business and just not know it yet. Business owners clean toilets, wash windows, set up computer systems, bring their lunches to work, and complete a host of other chores most would consider to be beneath the business owner, at least during the infancy stage of the business. Depending on the business type and industries served, the infancy stage can last from six months to three years. Beyond that, the model is not worth pursuing in most cases. This is an interesting concept. Let's expand on this.

II. Defining Failure.

What does a business look like when it has failed? Most of us immediately conjure up visions of empty desks, floors covered with scattered papers, maybe a picture or two hanging crooked on the wall, basically the aftermath of a typical office after it has completely gone out of business. Think again.

If you have gone through a business failure, you will have a completely different view of what a business looks like when it first flatlines. First of all, the full complement of employees is still working, still fulfilling their daily requirements. Remember, the brain continues long after the heart has stopped.

Unfortunately, most business owners are not trained to read EKGs or the business equivalents, profit and loss (P&L) and balance sheet statements. If you don't have working knowledge of what these statements report and how this information is interpreted, do yourself, your banker, your customers, and any mindless employees foolish enough to accept one of your paychecks a favor and go work for someone else. Don't even think of starting a business. You may argue that you know or knew someone who successfully ran a business for years and years without ever looking at a P&L or a balance sheet. To this I say, bull. While I'm sure this is the case in at least one successful enterprise in the history of the planet, this is by far the exception.

I personally knew of a few owners who could not read P&Ls and balance sheets but had wonderful equalizers, better known as accountants. These folks would create these statements, read them, and interpret what they were revealing and communicate this information clearly to the business owners. The owners would, in turn, then make the necessary course corrections to ensure success or at the very least sidestep disaster. Don't count on hiring one of these folks, however.

First of all, the good ones are few and far between. Sure, there are a lot of good CPAs when it comes to filing taxes and keeping you clear of the crosshairs of the IRS, but when it comes to interpreting P&Ls to the benefit of the business owner, well, let's just say you have your work cut out for you to even find a good CPA who can do this. If you do, you probably can't afford him. So the bottom line here is to learn how to read the bottom line yourself. It's not that hard.

Let's get back to what a business looks like when it fails. If you ask the average business owner to describe what his business would look like at flatline, the answer, after you get past the glazed-over eyes, will be shocking. Most owners do not have a clue what precedes the death pronouncement of their businesses. In other words, they do not truly know at what cash flow they would begin defaulting on their bills. They don't know what level of business they need to continue to achieve month in and month out in order to stay in the black. Most don't know if they are even in the black except for the ability to take a salary.

My recommendation is that when you are in the conceptualization phase of your entity, describe in great detail what the company will look like when it has failed. Define to the dollar what a minimum business level from clients will be. If you don't grow the business to this level within a predefined time period, it's time to bail. What will your minimum monthly cash flow look like? If you don't hit it a year down the road, close up shop. I have found that many business owners hang on to a losing business model like it is one of their children on life support. They just don't have the heart to pull the plug. If you define failure ahead of time, it will make this decision so much easier. Remember, failure in business, while undesirable, usually produces a successful business owner on the second or third attempt. This isn't high school. Being held back a year can be a really good thing.

How many of you have seen a business owner struggle year after year and then finally make it big? Not too many, I bet. It's been my experience that few finally make it. Most struggle the majority of their working careers in a business model that is widely flawed. I would estimate one in thirty-five finally make it on a large enough scale to justify the lean years. Most would have been much better off to admit failure and move on to a better business model. Eking out a living and owning a job is not the definition of success you have in mind when you start your business. Starting with failure in mind, as odd as it sounds, will help to ensure success in the next business while preserving your sanity in wrestling with the current business. Delaying the acceptance of failure only ensures prolonged failure. So how do we define failure?

The problem with defining failure long after the business has started is that it allows for the growth of burgeoning bias to flourish. The business is too close to our hearts for us to admit it has gone bad. We still want to hold its hand while the straps of the business world's electric chair are being buckled. Going down with the ship may be honorable at sea, but it's just plain goofy in the business world. Bring your talents, and bruised ego, to bear on a new business model. Your conscience, family, friends, clients, and the entire business community will be glad you did. Define failure first. You will be surprised how much more clearly you will define success.

III. Dues are paid with decision, both good and bad.

We are wired to be right all the time (unless you're a meteorologist). In the business world, if you are not making bad decisions, you are not making any decisions. Being correct on every decision every day of the week, week in and week out, is statistically impossible. I have made more than two hundred decisions in a single business day (I actually kept track during a particularly *robust* time period). Whether in the business environment or your personal life, you would be hard-pressed to find anyone who has made two hundred decisions in a row all correctly. Some of the folks I have worked with have barely been able to string together three correct decisions, and their personal lives reflected it. Since we are such flawed individuals, how are we to survive, much less thrive, as business owners? After all, making decisions on which clients to offer credit to has vastly more implications and repercussions than the average selection of a dinner entrée.

Regarding poor decision making and its implications in the business world, let me offer two examples of horrible decisions that had lasting positive effects. Both Steven Spielberg and Gene Roddenberry owe a debt of gratitude to poor decision making. The latter is to a lesser degree but still worth mentioning here.

Gene Roddenberry was the creator of *Star Trek*, and if you didn't know that, shame on you. The characters on *Star Trek*—Captain Kirk, Mr. Spock, Dr. McCoy, et al.—would travel the far reaches of space aboard the *Star Ship Enterprise*, and if you didn't know that either, shame on you again. As the *Enterprise* would approach a planet, the starship would begin to orbit the planet. The crew members selected to physically land on the planet would not use the *Enterprise*. Instead, they would use a smaller craft called a shuttle (the space equivalent of using a dinghy to come ashore from a large ship), or so it was originally planned. Unfortunately, the company hired to make the shuttle model was having difficulties in doing so. Roddenberry could not stop shooting, so he decided that the manner in which the crew members would be transported to the planet's surface would be via a device called a transporter.

The transporter would scramble the molecules of the human body being transported and then reassemble them on the surface of the planet. This was a truly brilliant alternative to the shuttle, or lack thereof, and one of *Star Trek's* signature technologies. An additional benefit of the transporter was that it did not involve any expensive props, which was important to a show watching its budget. I ask you, would *Star Trek* be the same without the Transporter Room? Hardly, but I still would have watched it. The poor decision in selecting the company to manufacture the shuttle model paid off in spades. If the company had made the shuttle model on schedule as originally promised, transporting would have one less meaning today and *Star Trek* would not be the same.

Steven Spielberg has been the director of many movies, as you may be aware, but his big break came when he took the director's chair on the set of *Jaws*. The movie made Spielberg an instant millionaire and afforded him great latitude in future projects. Quite the accomplishment for the thirty-year-old virtually unknown director.

The success of this horror movie was staggering. It possessed the ability to draw the viewer into the circumstances of the scenes almost to the point where he could taste the salt water. The reason behind the success is arguable, but the one standout feature of the film is the shark. Or should I say the shark's absence? Seeing a sixteen-foot shark capable of ripping open boats and dragging fishing piers out to sea is frightening. However, not seeing the animal capable of these feats is far more horrifying.

Why did we see so little of the shark? Was it brilliance on Spielberg's part? Could it have been the director's talents in the making? Well...not really. The shark couldn't swim. Or at least, the technical folks responsible for the shark could not make it swim. Some sources admitted that it was a challenge just to keep the damn thing from sinking. Consequently, Spielberg decided to use just a dorsal fin mock-up, and even that was used sparingly. What we didn't see was far more frightening than the actual shark. Poor decisions in hiring the crew who managed the shark led to success beyond imagination.

Stories such as these are rampant among the business world's industries, not just the entertainment world. Poor decisions in chemical selections led to Teflon, Post-it notes, and Super Glue. Countless other inventions happened through a series of poor decisions, one lying upon the other until the solution, many times the solution to an entirely different problem, became glaringly apparent.

Lack of proper planning coupled with disastrous decisions has led to several success stories in my own businesses. Some of my finest hours were preceded by some of my silliest mistakes. I have, at times, made snap decisions in situations where there just wasn't a good, clear decision and all avenues looked bleak, hoping the snap decision would shake out several issues. This in turn, it was hoped, would leave a smaller number of potholes to dodge. This may be a risky maneuver, but it is very effective when done with the strength of experience.

Poor decisions are part of business. Making lemonade from lemons, I'm sure, was also an accident of some sort. Many times, the mistake becomes the solution, or the solution to the mistake unearths the diamond just beneath the surface of the problem. One can only hope that the poor decision, once committed, is correctable with a pen stroke. Otherwise, the implications can be severe. This is especially true in the industries where corrections involve far more than just a pen stroke and money; they also involve labor—industries such as manufacturing and construction as opposed to, say, the service industries.

After making a poor decision in the financial industries, for example, the correction involves pen and paper and usually a monetary fee in order to "undo" the "do" and make things right. In the manufacturing and construction worlds, a poor decision also involves pen, paper, and money, but there is another element to consider: labor. A poor decision may not be able to be corrected with a pen stroke and a transfer of cash. Corrections may involve countless hours of labor. Let's look at an example.

A large appliance manufacturer is in the midst of producing a line of refrigerators. Your company supplies a widget that goes deep inside the bowels of those refrigerators. Weeks after the first units have arrived on customers' kitchen floors, it is discovered that your widget is breaking. The new supplier of raw material that you selected shipped the wrong grade of material. Clearly this was a bad decision on your part and the part of your new supplier.

Now, you can write the correction to the fridge manufacturer so they have assurance that you will not make this mistake again. And you can write the fridge manufacturer a big check covering all of the expenses. But this will not fix the problem. The fix will involve countless hours of labor taking apart the brand-new refrigerators and replacing your old widget with your new widget. The fix is just not implemented with pen, paper, and a check. There is a time element, a big one.

If you work or plan on working in a labor-related industry, how important is getting each decision correct? What if poor decisions cost lives? Replace the refrigerators with heart monitors. Now how paralyzed are you going to be when making even the simplest of decisions? Remember, we are conditioned by our schooling to not make mistakes so that when we get the test back from Mrs. Teacher, we have a perfect score. What if for each wrong answer we had to wash and wax the classroom floor? Strip and rewax, strip and rewax, for each wrong answer. I think even fewer entrepreneurs would exist today.

The point here is that we, as business owners, must be willing to rewax as many floors as we can. It is in this willingness—the willingness to make a bad call and pay the price for the correction—that we learn how to repair the fridge with as few movements as possible. I once heard the CEO of a Fortune 100 manufacturer tell one of his suppliers, "Every manufacturer breaks windows. We hire the ones that can repair them the fastest." This was true brilliance. He realized that everyone is eventually going to screw up, and in manufacturing, all the money in the world might not be able to fix the mistake. It takes a certain level of creativity to overcome some of these errors. And the folks who can recover the fastest are the guys he wanted on his team of suppliers.

If you aren't making decisions, you aren't making mistakes, and if you're not making mistakes, you will never learn the corrections that leave the fewest scars. In the business world, a few failing test scores early in your career are worth hundreds of perfect scores. Try explaining this to the academic world.

Let me give you one more brain bender. I know of a company in the Upstate New York area that has an unusual hiring process. The company provides forged parts to numerous industries. Now this product line is fairly technical. Their sales force must be equally technical in nature, so their first choice for new hires are degreed mechanical engineers. You might expect that the grades required to be considered for such a job would be rather high. If so, you would be dead wrong.

This company realized that engineers with very high grades tended to be far too introverted for sales positions. After all, what good is a salesman, even a technically capable one, if he is afraid to talk to his customers? The solution? Hire engineers with a GPA of 2.0 to 2.5. They have the wherewithal to understand the technical, even though they may not have the ability to be top-notch designers. They do, however, usually possess personality characteristics synonymous with successful salesmen. They tend to be much more gregarious, playful, and magnetic. This became policy for this New York company and has been successful. Why do I mention this?

How many times do you have to be wrong to earn a GPA of 2.0? By my calculations, I would assume three in ten. How many times have you heard of a target grade range of 2.0 for success? Can this translate into the entrepreneurial world? These new hires can understand the technical but are also quite personable. Is that a recipe for success? Bear in mind, the technical savvy is rarely complemented by shrewd business acumen, and a shrewd business mind is rarely accompanied by technical ability.. How potentially valuable is the "crossover"?

I do not want to undersell a 2.0 in engineering. I realize a 2.0 in most accredited collegiate engineering programs is equivalent to a 3.0 to a 3.5 in an awful lot of other majors, but it is still a 2.0. This is hardly cause for academic back-patting. It may just very well be cause for an entrepreneurial appointment, however. Academically, this may be the perfect entrepreneur.

Most 4.0 students make lousy business owners, regardless of their academic majors and/or pursuits.

You are asking someone on a daily basis to make multiple mistakes, at least in the early stages of business. This same person has been ingrained by our educational system to never make mistakes. He will either begin to refuse to make decisions, what is referred to as analysis paralysis, or implode mentally from the realization of his constant failures. In either case, I believe it to be quite clear that a 4.0 student probably does not have the best background for the entrepreneurial world.

Let me finish with a story of the outgoing president of a prestigious Ivy League university and his conversation with his successor. The newly appointed president asked his experienced colleague if he had any words of wisdom as he was about to embark on his retirement. The crafty old president nodded and said, "Be kind to your B students as they will come back and work as administrators. Take care of your A students as they will come back to teach. But take special note of your C students." The new president was taken aback by this and could not help but ask why special attention should be given to C students. The retiring president merely said, "They will come back and build your new buildings."

He had been president for many, many years and had come to realize that C students are the future's business owners. If you were the new president, where would you place your attention?

Underachievers rejoice!

IV. How are good decisions made?

Make decisions from the same gut instinct every time—your odds of making better decisions will increase. When faced with any decision, make sure you first ask yourself whether this is your decision to make. If it is not your decision, make sure the person who owns the decision makes it.

If it is your decision, next ask if the decision is reversible. Reversible decisions can be made quickly. Irreversible decisions, "bomb-dismantling decisions," require more time. You're down to two wires, red and blue; cut the wrong one and boom! If you don't make any decision, boom! Not all decisions are at the level of "bomb dismantling." Always take extra time with bomb decisions and try to not spend bomb time and energy on decisions that offer little bang.

Always write a quick note about why you made any major decision. Telephone Company A repeatedly screwed up billing and consequently overcharged on a regular basis. This was too time consuming. You went with Telephone Company B because it was the lesser of two evils. No decision will be correct forever. Timeliness is critical. A good decision today is far better than a great decision tomorrow.

V. Paging Dr. Reality...

"The second the light turns green, I'm going to cross the street." You cross, and a truck trying to make the yellow ends up running the red light and hits you. You were right. You're also dead; congratulations. The better decisions usually entail a reality check against the real world, and herein lies a big monster. So few new business owners and non-business owners know anything of how the real world actually works; their right-and-wrong mentality has no compass to guide it. Let me give you an example.

Recently, I was speaking to a schoolteacher regarding prescription drugs and the pharmaceutical companies that make them. The discussion moved toward the larger pharmaceutical companies and the value of their stock. A couple of firms in particular had increasing stock values over the last few years, and her explanation for this was that many baby boomers were now starting to age and this large demographic were buying these stocks because they needed the drugs these companies were manufacturing. This in turn was driving the stock values up. I really didn't know where to begin to refute such an outlandish statement. So much of her fundamental logic was so wrong. It was like trying to argue what chicken tastes like with someone who has never had a bucket of extra crispy.

Individual baby boomers, as an investment class, don't buy enough stock to make individual stock pricing rise. Even if they did, stock traders on the whole never ever buy stocks because they personally consume the products the company sells. Even if this were true, there are so many other things that can go wrong with an organization that would cause a stock price to drop even if underlying sales were climbing. I could go on here ad infinitum, but you get the picture. Her statement could not be more wrong.

Starting a business with this poor of an understanding of even the most fundamental workings of the markets, stocks and otherwise, can spell disaster. My best recommendation is to read at least the front page of the *Wall Street Journal* every day and take in at least one generic television business news show every other day. Stay away from the political shows for these purposes, however.

This advice is valid for even the most seasoned entrepreneur. Knowledge is power, and news concerning Fortune 50 companies actually has bearing on you and your business. For instance, such news can have a direct effect in the case where a Fortune 50 company has fired an advertising agency. This impacts you because that advertising agency is your largest customer. Or such news can have an indirect effect in the case where a Fortune 50 company is faced with the same type of decision that you are facing but on a larger scale. The news article covers what decision they made and how the problem was solved. Remember, all business decisions are the same across all businesses, large and small. The only thing that really changes is the scale of the decision. Can either of these help you? Count on it.

Your goal is to broaden your horizons from the experiences of others. A wise man learns from others. A fool has to piss on the electric fence himself.

VI. Characteristics of Successful Business Owners

Our genetic wiring many times determines whether we will succeed in business. Take a test of your weather vane. Are you more concerned about the promotion of the business itself or the happiness of each individual employee? Would you be able to move forward knowing that the business will only succeed if one of your employees is always miserable? Is the most important thing in owning a business waking up and being completely elated to go to work? Or is the financial success more important? So much in today's media depicts business owners as heartless SOBs when in reality the business owner is required by the very nature of the business environment to make decisions based solely on survival rather than emotion.

Wouldn't it be wonderful if you could give your employees everything they ever asked for and still had enough left over to make the business a success?

If you actually answered this question, I suggest you come back down to earth. A seasoned business owner would have begun to shake his head long before the question was half asked. Hone your skills in thinking logically.

There are certain character traits that make owning and operating a business much more likely to be successful. Let's look at some of the keys to business. These are the items you must have a grip on.

i. Math.

I intentionally placed this one first. Without a firm understanding of math, you cannot understand finances, period. Math is the only subject taught in school that stands on its own. By this I mean it is the only subject that has few to no gray areas. It is 100 percent right or wrong and cannot be taught with any bias. There are no liberal or conservative math books. Math is the same the world over and is the only universal world language. There are ways of surviving, even excelling, in business without a firm understanding of literature, history, geography, and the like. These subjects may be helpful, but I can assure you that without a firm grip on at least the very basics of math, you are almost destined for failure.

If you don't have a grip on math, someone else will have a grip on your money, if you're lucky enough to ever come to own any. The only prayer you have is to have someone in your life whom you truly trust to handle your finances, someone who, in the end, doesn't rip you off. How many stories have we heard of professional athletes who, having only a fifth-grade understanding of math, lost their fortunes to unscrupulous agents and personal managers? Unscrupulous agents, managers, etc., stole funds from these athletes on a regular basis and in "broad daylight" without the athletes having a clue.

A fool and his money are lucky enough to get together in the first place. In our case, a fool is someone who does not understand math and, consequently, finances. Remember, finances are fairly easy, if you understand math. If you were one of the multitudes to go through their primary education lacking fundamental math skills, go back and get them. And by go back I don't mean to high school. There are unlimited resources online to get you up to speed at least to the Algebra I level.

No excuses exist here. "I'm a girl, and girls don't understand math" and "I just don't get it" don't fly. Keep trying until it makes sense. Success in the business world, scratch that, success in life is damn near impossible without some fundamental math skills. I have seen business owners who read and write on a third-grade level become multimillionaires. Their math skills were at least tenth grade. And I don't mean remedial tenth grade.

ii. Risk.

This should actually be labeled "low risk-averse." This is a paradigm of sorts. Successful business owners tend to be better savers than non-business owners but at the same time are not averse to taking risks. Another way to say this is they tend to save their chips in one big pile but are not afraid to let the whole thing ride on just one number, just one bet. The difference between this behavior and that of a reckless gambler is like night and day.

The difference between this behavior and that of a pack of wild dogs in Africa is like night and a little later that night. When you find a business owner willing to bet it all, you usually find wounded prey and a dozen or so of the owner's operatives moving in for the kill. The business owner is willing to make the bet when the opportunity arises and the odds are heavily in his favor. That willingness is the key ingredient that is missing in non-business owners. Being aware of your level of risk aversion, especially if your level to risk aversion is low, is critical to success in the business world. When the iron is hot, you gotta hit the damn thing.

iii. Sociability.

Tom, Dick, and Harry—you need to know at least two out of the three. Do you feel your stature and place in society are too lofty to say hello to the rabble? If you identify with and can relate to such a feeling of stature, your ego is going to get in the way of your business success. Business owners almost to a fault tend to be outgoing and gregarious. They will "chat" with almost anyone. Not because they have deep desires to make new friends but because they never know who these other people are, what business potential they represent, and who they know and what business potential they represent. You cannot walk around like you are two weeks into a six-year Senate seat. It would be much better to walk around like you have only two weeks left on a six-year Senate seat.

iv. Perception.

This one is almost impossible to teach, and some will argue this until they are blue in the face. Here is the concept: it does not matter what color the sky actually is; it only matters what color your clients EXPECT it to be. Going into business to make a political statement is not a business model. It is a political statement. If you have ever heard an angry audience yelling, "Shut up and sing" to a performer, you will understand what I mean. Save the superiority speeches for the family dinner table.

They do not belong in the world of business, unless your business is politics.

If you are the type of person who insists on crossing the street the second the light changes, you will have a very hard time with this concept as well. You are more likely to stick with the "I am right" perception rather than the "I know it is wrong for drivers to run the red light, but I get to live if I wait a few more seconds before I cross" perception. Insisting on any action purely because you feel morally right or amorally right or immorally right is suicidal in the business world. Congratulations, you are right. You are also dead, but you are, or should I say were, right. We'll be sure to put it on your headstone.

I see more liberals having problems with this than conservatives, if this helps you see where you land on this character trait. I will use the Iraq war as an example here. The liberal argument is that the war was started over incorrect information. We should have never invaded Iraq to begin with, and consequently, we should leave immediately. The conservative argument is that regardless of the information that led up to the invasion, we are there now and must see it to a successful completion. I need only ask you which outcome allows your business to have more opportunity for success? A further disorganized Iraq and the high probability of expensive energy or the potential for a democratic ally in Iraq? If you get this answer wrong, please rethink the whole "I want to be in business" idea. (Also please bear in mind, I couldn't care less what your political ideology is here. My only concern is your mind-set in preparation for success in your entrepreneurial career. I don't have time for political demagoguery; I have entrepreneurial demands instead, and so should you if you value success.)

v. Assertiveness.

If you prefer a backseat position, well off the radar of responsibility, stay on the W-2 path. If your brain begins to buckle when it comes time to take the lead, put your reputation on the line, and take on ultimate responsibility, you are probably not wired for owning your own business. Successful entrepreneurs live for this responsibility. They always want the ball, sometimes to a fault. Remember, I am not passing judgment here. I am merely pointing out what I have seen to be common among successful entrepreneurs. I am sure there have been success stories where the owner was less than eager to take on a leadership role. But wouldn't you guess these would be few and far between?

Chapter 2

The Experts

I. Economists and the random walk theory

This theory is really quite simple. It states that a stock at any given moment in time has just as much likelihood to go up as it has likelihood to go down. If you take this theory on a minute-by-minute basis, it is probably correct to some degree, but not even day traders work on this minute-by-minute time scale. Overall, I can't tell you how much I disagree with this theory, not only from a market perspective but also because of the implications that it has in the independent world of business. More on this in a minute.

If we look at some of the better money managers who, on a monthly basis, yearly basis, month in, month out, year in, year out, continue to make money, how can we explain the random walk theory? It doesn't hold up. There is no way to explain how someone can continue to be successful over and over and over if the theory is to be supported. It just will not sustain scrutiny. There are money managers out there who are rarely, if ever, negative at the end of the year. I personally know money managers who throughout the 2008 and 2009 calendar years made money. How is this possible?

It's possible because they simply are that good. The systems that they follow tell them when to get in, when to get out, and what plays to make when they are in. Their systems work. It's that simple.

These are the same folks who will tell you that diversification of your money is a hedge against ignorance. That is a very important statement. Many people in the financial world will call me flat-out arrogant for making such a statement. But if you truly had a system that worked, why would you put money into a bunch of different stocks, bonds, mutuals, etc. that only had a random chance of an uptick when you had a 51 percent chance of an uptick with a good system? Note, here I am only using 51 percent. If the random walk is just 50 percent, then a 51 percent system is going to be more successful.

Now let's translate this into the business world, and instead of a stock or a bond, let's say that someone, maybe a bank, is going to buy into YOU. No, this is not a new stock symbol. I am referring to you personally. If, as many economists proclaim, the business world, much like the random walk theory, is simply luck and those who are successful merely won life's lottery, can we say that you and your skills are at least 1 percent better than a flip of a coin? Do you believe in yourself enough to gain 1 percent, 3 percent, 10 percent, 20 percent, 50 percent on a coin flip? Gary Player, the famous golfer, once stated, "The harder I practice, the luckier I get." I would say that half of the 50 percent in the coin flip is just showing up. What do the SATs give you for just showing up and taking the test? This is a good metaphor for the business world in America. Just starting a business is worth something. The rest is hard work and preparations.

Do you see how ridiculous it would be to blatantly say that business owners who are successful—and I have heard economics professors say this—are so due to mere chance? With only one in four, one in five, or one in six businesses making it past the five-year mark, I would say that a fifty-fifty chance is rather overstated. If it were mere chance, damn near everyone I know would be doing this. No, success in the business world is not managed merely by fate. To quote Einstein, "God does not play dice with the universe." And success in the business world goes far beyond anything "random."

Let's look at it like this. Bill Gates could not believe IBM handed him their PC's disk operating system (DOS). The disk operating system that runs every PC was just handed to him. You may call that fortunate. But let's look at this a bit closer.

Would this have happened if Mr. Gates had stayed in school and not started Microsoft? Did he only show up? Far from just showing up, he was prepared to understand what IBM obviously did not understand: DOS was highly valuable. Was he just lucky? Even today, some thirty years later, if IBM handed DOS to some schmo on the street, would he recognize what he had been given? I would guess no. Would you recognize this if it were given to you today? This goes eons beyond just luck.

First and foremost, Bill Gates had to start Microsoft. Second, Microsoft had to have developed a track record large enough for IBM to recognize it as a viable source to develop their DOS package. Third, Bill Gates had to have the wherewithal to recognize what DOS truly offered his company—he could have passed on this opportunity thinking it was not worth his time. Last, he had to have the know-how to write DOS as a working software package—not an easy feat. Where the hell do you see "and then a miracle occurred and Bill became a billionaire" in the above statements? This was born of Bill Gates and his partners. If you can blame his success on luck, then I can blame misspelled words on my pencil.

There are companies out there that can use your business's capabilities right now. I'm referring to the business that you have not created yet. Your business is you. All of the products and services that your business offers are you, and there are companies out there that need you.

Just showing up with your skills satisfies those demands. Half the battle is won. The remainder is managing the business so that it makes a profit at the end of the day. Where in all of that did you hear me say, "And then lightning will strike and you will be rich"? Random? Highly unlikely in my opinion. But you now possess more knowledge than the PhDs who will mock your success. That's OK; you can splash mud on their Priuses as you pass them in your BMW. Now you need only the courage to investigate what services you can offer and what skills you possess to support those services.

II. Earning your stripes.

Business is designed to have you fail at least a hundred times. You will need to earn your stripes over and over again. Sheepskins are not recognized in the business world. This is one of the main reasons there is a disdain between the entrepreneurial world and academia. After all, in the realm of academics there is a natural progression towards esteem, admiration, and possible fame. In the realm of the entrepreneurial world, there is only one step: did you make money or not? It is as black-and-white as you can get, which is another nail in the coffin for half the academic world that deals in liberal arts since nothing is black-and-white. Nothing is abhorred more by most entrepreneurs than gray areas. Are you seeing the multitude of conflicts?

In the end, academics achieve undergrad status, followed by master's-level status, followed by doctorate-level status, and on to being published, again and again. All of this to reach six-figure income levels. Not bad when considering the workload, but most entrepreneurs would gladly work many more hours for the potential for more income. The goal in mind for the business owner is to absorb the initial costs and pay out the salaried and hourly folks, while not taking any income for long periods of time—all for the golden goose at the end of the rainbow. Mixed metaphors aside, this is mainly viewed as reckless by the academic mind as there is little security in this approach.

Remember, the academic mind needs the backing of the large institution as a source of income. Academics are not risk takers and may never become such. Imagine the horror of "gambling" your entire income on one paper. If you're published, you are paid; if not, you go hungry. How many professors do you think would go for this? I can't think of one that I had that would be willing to do so. Most of the PhDs I had in college were wound so tight financially that if you stuck a piece of coal up their butts, in an hour you would have a diamond—and they were the liberal profs. Bear in mind, these folks are more than glad to show you pictures of them getting stoned at Woodstock and screaming obscenities at Lyndon Johnson but somehow become J. Edgar Hoover when it comes to taking risks with their checking accounts. I don't even want to begin to describe the business and engineering professors I had.

I once saw an engineering professor call for maintenance because a coffee vending machine did not give him his nickel in change. Would you expect a business owner to do something like this? Here is the key to this concept, so pay attention. The academic says, "The machine did not give me my five cents, and this is wrong. So I will call maintenance to retrieve it." The business owner says, "The machine ripped me off, so I will not use this machine in the future. Calling maintenance will take at least thirty minutes out of my day, if I'm lucky. If I make more than ten cents an hour, I cannot justify spending thirty minutes trying to get five cents back, not to mention the wasted time of the maintenance man." One is right but loses. One is wrong but wins. Applying this to the day-in, day-out practices of the business owner's world, you can see how the academic will spend dollars chasing dimes, whereas the entrepreneur will spend dimes retrieving dollars. Again, if you don't get this, please put this book down and step away from the W-9. Seriously.

Let's look at another example. In my first job out of school, I worked with a true academic at heart, except for the fact that he barely finished his undergrad. Apparently he had a little trouble with math—a minor issue to the average ECONOMICS major. Any who, he was describing his utter contempt for hunting and how barbaric he felt it was. (Just as a side note, I couldn't care less if you are a member of the NRA or a member of PETA. Keep your political views to yourself; the issue here is whether you will survive the business world.) He then began to describe how that weekend he planned on walking into the woods, in a part of the country that is known for deer hunting, and threatening any deer hunter he stumbled across. Since he did not believe in gun ownership, I just could not resist asking the obvious question: "You are going to threaten a deer hunter with your bare hands? A deer hunter that is carrying a high-powered rifle and probably a high-powered handgun as well?" Carrying a sidearm is common in that part of the country in case the deer is not killed quickly by the rifle. "Are you aware of the potential danger to your life in threatening a hunter, who, if your descriptions are correct, is either too drunk or too stupid to live?" He replied, "If that hunter levels a rifle at me, he had better use it." From what I have seen from most of the hunters I have met, not only will they use it, they will boast to all of their friends about how far they separated your ass from your armpits.

Quick check: are you right now thinking, "Well yes, but then the hunter will go to jail"? If so, you are still missing the point of this book. Being right and dead means you lose. And no, I do not feel that threatening hunters is right. If you feel a moral obligation to stop hunting and feel you are right, I can truly understand this. But can you see, regardless of if this person is morally right, where he is going wrong? The light has changed, and I am going to cross the street this instant, and I don't care if there is traffic coming. Best of luck in your new career as a hood ornament for a Peterbilt—a Peterbilt undoubtedly being driven by a deer hunter. Vaya con dios.

By the way, from time to time while reading this book you may hear a popping sound. You may be experiencing *headius rectus retrievus*. I really don't think I need to explain this.

III. Fame is famous for fouling fortune

I can honestly say I have never met a business owner whose first intent was fame. If fame is your target, put this book down and start taking acting classes or, at the very least, start waiting tables. The only reason the famous are famous is because of the mainstream media, and there is little else the mainstream media despises more than the small business owner. You would have better luck getting 60 Minutes to do a puff piece on Wal-Mart. After all, you, as a successful business owner, have circumvented the world of academia, the world of mass media, and the world of pop culture, and have become equally if not vastly more wealthy than all of the latter without worshiping at their altars or, more importantly, contributing to their coin trays. This just is not done.

Please don't misunderstand; I am a firm believer in a college education. I believe in getting a balanced daily dose of the news. I believe in being entertained by the entertainers. However, I am not foolish enough to allow myself to be lectured by the entertainers. I am not addle enough to believe the entertainment that is cast by most anchors. And I certainly am not small enough to be cast into social stations by educators. If you allow yourself to be handled in such ways, you have stripped yourself of the ability to define who you are. Fame entails being liked for the most part. This is a strong emotion and flies in the face of logical decision making. If you seek fame and the satisfaction of being liked, you relinquish your capacity to seek fortune separate from fame.

In the eyes of academia, entertainment, and pop culture, successful small business owners have simply won the lottery. After all, you did not spend years sitting in classes and writing a doctorial thesis, spend years trying to be discovered at that tiny local news station, or do a dozen or more incontinence commercials to finally have made a name for yourself as a serious actor. You can afford the same first-class plane ticket, and you didn't even have to narrowly escape plagiarism on your master's paper, overcome the malicious accusations on the news piece that sent you national, or dodge the porn industry. You too can afford the presidential suite at the Plaza, the box seats at the Met, the hidden bungalow on Bora-Bora's north shore. How in the hell is this possible? You are the undeserving, the great unwashed. Business owners are not part of this elite. My response to this has always been, "More the pity." You need only to acknowledge that you see the difference and get back to what you do. They shall never be you, and you shall never be them. Just be aware that this group will never do you any favors.

Chapter 3

The Forces from Without

I. Governmental Intervention

What are you up against? The forces from without. Aside from the innate issues (the forces from within) surrounding the successful management of a business, there are other forces that can, even with the most brilliant business platforms, inflict disaster. I speak, of course, of government intervention. How your business is taxed and regulated can have moderate to profound effects on your profitability to say the very least. To say the very most, it can have profound effects on your very survival. Am I stating that the government can destroy your business? Without question, the government can and does destroy businesses.

Let's hit upon just a few examples to give you an idea of how this happens. In the mid 1980s, there were dozens of small businesses in the real estate industry doing quite well. One of the reasons properties were moving was that there was a favorable tax law allowing for large deductions on tax returns for losses on passive investments. Many individuals as well as small to large companies were taking advantage of this tax law and buying property, such as rental property, that was losing money. The deduction law was such that it made financial sense to own losing properties. As you can imagine, the real estate business was booming as a result of this law.

Then came the Tax Reform Act of 1986. This reversed the tax advantages in owning these underperforming properties. It didn't take a genius to see a real estate crash coming when this law changed. And, boy, did it crash. You may remember this as the S&L crisis, but for the purposes of this book, I am not going to get into many of the ancillary issues that surrounded this crisis. The reason for discussing the crisis is simply this: if you owned a real estate brokerage or if you were simply an agent working as an independent contractor, your world was going to change by the end of fiscal '86.

You may argue that the tax law as it was written should have never been there and no one should have been allowed to take advantage of this law in the first place. (Once again, I couldn't care less what your politics are or were.) Remember, I stated "one" of the reasons properties were moving was due to this favorable law. This was not the *only* reason. However, the crash happened *solely* because of this tax law change. Do you see the distinction here?

A tax loophole helped real estate businesses to some degree, but a tax change destroyed real estate businesses in totality. If you owned a real estate brokerage or were just a real estate agent, you were not necessarily participating in the tax favorability. You were simply selling real estate. But the government changing the tax law destroyed your business because it destroyed your entire industry.

Economies, as I'm sure you have realized, are self-fulfilling prophecies. If everyone tells you an industry is going to drop, whether it is healthy or not, it is going to drop. And this is exactly what happened to the real estate industry at that time.

Let's look at another example. Imagine, if you will, you started a small company that supplies a certain type of chemical to the tungsten industry. (To save you the trouble of looking it up, tungsten is a very hard, very heat-resistant element also known as wolfram.) Your chemical aids in the manufacturing of wire tungsten, to be specific. Uses are diverse as tungsten is used in everything from vacuum tubes to nozzles on rocket engines, from electron microscopes to the tips used in darts. However, most of the wire tungsten market is consumed by one single solitary industry. So strong is this industry that more than 70 percent of the tungsten wire is consumed by this one industry. If you make tungsten wire, this is your main customer base. What is this one industry, you may ask. Lightbulbs, of course. Lightbulb elements (the part of the lightbulb that actually lights up) are made from tungsten wire and have been for the past hundred years. Apparently, according to our government, one hundred years is long enough.

Imagine yourself spending years developing a chemical that aids in producing and refining tungsten wire, thinking and knowing the only competitors to the incandescent bulb are ten times the price and environmentally unsafe. (I refer to the mercury in compact fluorescent bulbs that if thrown away will leach into our drinking water through landfills.) "No one in their right mind will pay eight dollars for one lightbulb," you think to yourself. LED bulbs are even more expensive than fluorescent bulbs. The return on the investment of either compact fluorescent bulbs or

LEDs is five years or more. Why would anyone do this? Because the government made it law.

Now your small chemical business that you spent years developing is worthless. Well, not worthless; there still is that 30 percent remaining in business that is not related to the lighting industry. Unfortunately, it's not a large enough portion of business to pay the bills. The government's changes will destroy your business.

Now for the really important part. Let's change the real estate industry and the lightbulb industry to your industry—whatever industry you may work in currently. You say you're considering working for the government? If you are, why the hell are you reading this book? Even so, you are not protected. As I write this very page, California and New York are facing massive layoffs due to revenue shortfalls. So the government eats its own as well. Back to the industry you work in.

Regardless of what industry you may currently serve, you are not insulated. I rate the U.S. federal and state governments as the largest threat to any small business. This account is either in direct taxation and regulation as in the former Tax Reform Act of 1986 or indirect taxation and regulation as in our latter tungsten example above. Government rules and regulations are the most potentially damaging of all external business threats.

Remember, the government has a history of destroying entire industries, let alone single businesses. In ten years, the incandescent bulb in the U.S. will be about as obsolete as the electric trolley.

II. Renters and Sellers

Those evil rich people. What a phrase, huh? I did not grow up wealthy and am still a bit perplexed by the rich label being thrust upon me. I still do not consider myself to be rich, so let's define our terms. According to census statistics covering 2007, the median household income nationwide is hovering around $50,000. If we double this figure, and you land in the $100,000 yearly household income category, are you rich? I would say no, but you are somewhat comfortable. Let's increase the 2007 average by one "order of magnitude." For those of you who never sat in a physics class, one order of magnitude is ten. So we are saying that you are rich if you earn $500,000 per year. Are we safe in stating this? I don't believe so since my measure of wealth is directly related to the number of hours you MUST work per week to maintain your lifestyle. The operative word is *must*.

If that number is forty or more a week, you are poor, regardless of how much you earn. Do you understand this? This is so very important in grasping the true nature of wealth. True wealth is power. Why else would there be such a clamor around who has it, who doesn't have it, who will try to take it, etc.?

Power comes in the form of time. If you own your time, you own your life. CHOOSING to spend your time in a career as opposed to being REQUIRED in a MUST situation is entirely different. A MUST situation is where you are RENTING your time to a company in a W-2 format. If you CHOOSE to work, you can just as easily CHOOSE to spend your time watching paint dry. You would still OWN your life. RENTING your time is not the opposite of OWNING your time. The opposite of OWNING your time is SELLING your time. Your time is sold when you land on and stay on some form of government assistance. Your life, your soul, your vote, and your will have all been enslaved to that political power that so chooses to feed you—a child in an adult's body and completely POWERLESS. You have nothing.

So now we have our definitions. There are really then only three: those who OWN their time, those who RENT their time, and those who have SOLD their time. And while you can RENT for a considerable amount of time and become a very solid OWNER, you truly are not wealthy until you move from RENTING to OWNING. Basically, if you do not need to work, whether you work or not, you OWN your time. If you must work, you RENT your time. If you do nothing but cash someone else's checks in the form of government assistance, you are SOLD.

Now why did we go through all of this minutiae? Simple reasoning: the definitions of wealth are too ambiguous, too weak, and do not mirror reflection on oneself. I think you will agree that they do now. They are now too simple to be confused with each other. They are too well defined to be abused. And they are too crisp to allow us to ignore our own accomplishments as well as our own shortcomings.

Now let's look at an example of what you will be up against. I live in a fairly rural area, so much so that there was not an official town for the location of my subdivision. We were simply considered "county." The nearest town was small but quite slyly decided to begin to expand its borders in an effort to increase tax revenue. (Texas does not have income tax but makes up for this by having fairly high property taxes in the order of 2–3 percent of the total value of one's home.) By gobbling up more and more subdivisions, our neighboring town could easily increase revenues by a million dollars or more. The local town had an additional 0.6 percent city property tax that we who lived in the county were not paying. Not bad for a town of less than seven thousand people.

The downside for our subdivision was some of the more valuable homes could face additional property tax bills of $2,000 to $10,000 per year. Some of the smaller homes in our development were looking at an increase of $800 per year—not chump change but still a far cry from $2,000 and up. In an effort to stop the impending annexation, we decided to form our own town and held elections. The thought process was simple, or so I thought. Vote to incorporate our own little town and everybody in our subdivision wins. Right?

Wrong. Many of the smaller homeowners began to realize that the larger homeowners were about to save a lot more money in taxes. Quite true in that property taxes are a percentage of the value of one's home. The more expensive the home, the higher the property taxes and consequently the greater the savings potential if the taxes were averted. When sharing my views of pushing for incorporation of our little city, here is the response I received from one of the homeowners. I will let you decide if he is an OWNER, a RENTER, or SOLD:

"If it only affects the rich guy, i.e. like yourself, then I'm all for stickin' it to tha' man, if you catch my drift. You guys need to pay your share! Meanwhile we smaller homeowners shouldn't be expected to carry the brunt of the overwhelming financial burden our county is experiencing."

By incorporating into a small town, this individual was going to save a little over $900 a year in property taxes. However, he would rather pay the $900 if it would mean I was going to pay $5,000 in additional property taxes. This goes beyond remarkable. First of all, he ignored the fact that it was not going to only affect the "rich guy" and that he was going to have to pay a fair amount more in property taxes as well.

The emotional driver here was voiding my savings of $5,000. His additional taxes were almost irrelevant. Well hell, they *were* irrelevant; you read his e-mail excerpt above. His only concern was "stickin' it to tha' man." Couple this with his confusion over where these additional taxes would be spent. Remember, this was a city tax, and his concerns were rooted in "the overwhelming financial burden our *county* is experiencing."

I think you can judge from his comments that he is a RENTER. What's worse is that he has turned SELLER. He is retired and has no pension and little to no cash accumulation. His concerns are not of the well-being of his family or himself. His concerns revolve around making sure no one else is permitted to excel, to achieve, to flourish, beyond his own conceived notions.

Twenty years ago, I would not have believed that a person such as this existed. Ten years ago, I would have acknowledged such an existence but only as being few in number. Now I see this type of attitude proliferated throughout our country. I don't know if their numbers were always there or if they have grown over the decades. It really doesn't matter now, does it?

Let me share one more example. It's 11:58 a.m., and I am sitting in Mrs. Jones' fourth-grade class. We are about to be dismissed for recess. It's a beautiful May morning, and I am really looking forward to our upcoming football game on the playground. Mrs. Jones is working to quiet the thirty-eight nine-year-olds in her charge. Her repeated shouts of "Quiet!" are not really doing the trick. She announces that the next child who speaks will cost the entire class five minutes of recess time. Do you have any idea how much playground football can be lost in the span of five minutes?

Almost as soon as she says this, a classmate of mine opens his mouth. Then another and then another. By the time noon rolls around, we have lost twenty of the thirty minutes allotted for recess. While on the playground for our ten minutes of football, I stop for a second or two and notice something. Almost to a child, each and every classmate who spoke is just standing there. Sure, they might be talking with some other classmate, but by and large, they are not engaged in any physical activity. Recess for them might as well have been conducted in the classroom at their desks. Costing the entire classroom recess time really didn't cost them anything. What kind of adults do you think these children grow up to be? Let's fast-forward and go back to my small community in Texas.

The lake where I live is fairly large. There is roughly thirty miles of shoreline, and dozens of subdivisions back up to the lake's shoreline. The subdivisions vary from mobile homes to eight-figure mansions.

The property taxes in Texas are a rather contentious subject. They pay for city and county expenses, as you can imagine, and are roughly just under 1 percent of property value each year. Of more interest is the school tax that is lumped in with the property tax. School taxes can be well over 2 percent just in and of themselves. All combined, the taxes are roughly 2.7 percent of total property value each year. Not a small amount.

The percentage of this tax has been fought for many years by homeowners. It is thought of as an outrageously high tax by many homeowners. Unfortunately, most of these folks have been owners of fairly expensive homes, aka "tha' man." Even though this tax has been the same percentage for smaller homes as larger homes, the owners of the smaller homes in our county didn't seem to have a problem paying this outrageous percentage, until 2009.

You see, our little community has a problem. It has almost run out of lakefront land for new homes. Consequently, people have begun to buy up property in poorer neighborhoods, remove the mobile homes, and build larger, custom homes. This has driven the value of the property skyward. Some small tracts of land previously used for mobile homes have had values double and triple in the last three to four years.

All of a sudden, the property owners who have lived on the lake for twenty years or more have had their land value rise from $20,000 to well over $100,000. If I were in this position, I would be jumping for joy, but, much to my amazement, these folks are furious. They are furious with their tax bill, their *property* tax bill. What was once a yearly bill for $1,400 has more than doubled to almost $4,000. Why weren't they upset with their tax bill prior to this? It was the same percentage!

The answer is the percentage was the same, but the total value was grossly different. The percentages were fine when someone else was paying to educate every child in the community. It was OK to have excessive taxes when someone else was buying the new school bus as long as the small homeowners were only buying the muffler.

This sudden windfall that promoted these individuals' tax payments from minor to average was now an issue. Yes, the tax bill would be higher, but it would be higher because what they owned was that much more valuable. In the end, they did not want value. They simply did not want to play football on that playground. In the game of life, they have chosen to just stand there.

These folks are out there. They are renters and sellers and are not happy with windfalls in their own portfolios. They will have even less concern with your financial success. This is yet another force from without you will need to deal with since these folks drive, vote, and reproduce. Making entrepreneurial success that much more difficult will be in their every thought, word, and deed.

III. Sidestep the sexism.

If you're thinking of the glass ceiling, stop. There is no glass ceiling in entrepreneurialism. The success of a small business is not dependent upon your gender, and if you don't believe me, take a look at the following excerpt from U.S. News & World Report dated August 2007:

"There has never been a better time to be a woman with the entrepreneurial bug. Businesses owned by women are the fastest-growing sector of new ventures in the United States. Nearly half of all privately held firms in 2004 were at least 50 percent owned by women, according to the National Foundation for Women Business Owners. Between 1997 and 2004, the number of businesses owned by women grew by almost 20 percent, compared with only a 9 percent increase overall."

Clearly there has never been a better time for a female to "skirt" the sexual trap of the corporate world and truly display her talents. Females are entering the entrepreneurial world at a rate twice the national average. It is along these lines that I would like to suggest a business structure, and to do this, I am going to relate a personal story. So gather 'round, kids. Uncle Johnny is going to take you to a wonderfully wacky place called "the freak'n real world" and, boy, does it suck sometimes.

Many years ago when I was starting my importing company, it came to pass that our new firm was going to need capital. Like most new ventures, we did not have enough cash on hand to make it past the point of full return, also known as the point of critical mass. This basically means we could not get to the point where our organization could support itself long term. Our expenses were higher than our income, and we needed a few more months of cash infused into our coffers in order to reach this nirvana known as viability. (More on all of this when we discuss the internal issues, or forces from within.) Long story short, we needed some money. Dare I say it, but we needed a bank loan.

So off to the bank we went. We packed a small lunch, carefully removed our rectums and placed them in the company safe, and drove off to sit and chat with our local banker. If ever in my life I had felt like an insignificant little turd, this was it. We lacked three years of tax returns; yes, the lack of three years of tax returns as a minimum leads the list of offenses we brought to our banker. This means that if you can't show where you made money for at least the past three years, the bank will not even look at you. Can I just ask, if you can show where you made money for the past three years, WHAT THE HELL DO YOU NEED A BANK FOR? Sorry about that. Where was I? Oh yes, from our lack of tax returns to our lack of previous work experience (this one really pissed me off) to our lack of customers, we were nothing more than cannon fodder being repeatedly loaded and fired into small business oblivion by our "personal banker." This was a man who himself attempted to run several small businesses with no luck whatsoever. Chalk up three complete failures to Mr. Banker, and he was telling us what a successful entrepreneur should do. You might as well go back to college and ask a PhD. Actually, now that I think about it, I knew his speech sounded familiar.

Any who, after I cooled down a bit and coaxed the third vein off the ledge of my forehead, I thanked him for his time, and we were out the door of our friendly neighborhood bank.

By the way, the reason I was so pissed off at comments he made concerning our previous work experience was simply this: at the time of that interview, I had successfully managed (as a general manager) three organizations—two of which I took out of the red and into the black and a third I took from the mundane to the exceptional. All of these organizations were many times larger than our new venture. In addition, I had successfully started and grown a sales agency that I was voluntarily closing to help fund and start this new venture. My business partner, who owned the other half of this company, had lesser but very similar experience. Moreover, there was not a failure between us. To say the least, this was not our first rodeo.

Now, why do I say all of this? Well, let me introduce our next character. She was forty-eight years old and had worked in sales for a pharmaceutical company her entire professional life. She had a BA degree in PHYSICAL FITNESS, mind you, and ABSOLUTELY NO PRIOR EXPERIENCE RUNNING A COMPANY. She also had zero experience owning a company—not even a paper route as a child—nada, zip, nyet, nein, cipher, zilch. Got it? Great. And her selection of a business to start? Well, what is one of the most difficult businesses to manage successfully? You guessed it. She wanted to open a restaurant.

Oh and by the way, she happened to be my ex-business partner's sister-in-law. Since she had such little experience in the do-it-yourself business world, my ex-business partner was tutoring her. He had a first-row seat watching her grow as a small business owner. The order of instruction was typical: business plan, marketing plan, alternate plan, etc. After all of this came the discussion on funding. Since she had little funding of her own, her first trip was to, you guessed it, the bank.

I can still remember my ex-business partner's facial expression when he walked into my office after the meeting with the bank. Disbelief would be a gross understatement. It looked like he had just witnessed Al Gore proclaim it global cooling day by setting the Redwood National Park ablaze with an aerosol can and a Zippo.

"She got the loan," he uttered. My reply was simple: "Are you sh!##!^& me?" Now, don't get me wrong; she is a wonderful person. She is bright, articulate, and has a wonderful sense of humor. However, the bank that gave her $250,000 was not dating her. They had proclaimed her someone of business savvy and entrepreneurial worth. How much worth? Exactly a quarter of a million dollars. Her lending institution was the same bank that would not lend us a single penny. Two gentlemen with thirty plus years of successful experience and engineering degrees were not good enough. But a physical fitness major trying to now fry an omelet with no experience whatsoever was somehow worth $250K.

We had the right idea in removing something from our anatomy before going to visit the banker.

We were just off by an inch or two in our removal selection, if you get my drift. It would appear that there are special provisions within lending institutions that favor minorities. And females are considered a minority. The lesson here? If at all possible, put the business in your wife's name.

If you're a female entrepreneur, take one step ahead of the class. If you're not, this is just another force from without that you will have to deal with.

IV. The media elite.

This one may sound odd; after all, what can the media elite do to the small business owner? The answer is: put you out of business. First case in point is *The Oprah Winfrey Show*. It was mid-January 2009, and Oprah's guest was Suze Orman. They were discussing money-saving techniques during the recession of '09, and there were many tips being given, such as don't use your credit card for a week, don't spend cash for a day, and don't go out to eat for a month...what?!? Did they say not to go to a restaurant for an entire month? No, I'm not kidding all you folks in the restaurant business; they said a month. Distributors, truck drivers, busboys, advertising specialists, etc.—all of you were attacked. Your business was put on hold for thirty days—zero income. Oprah asked her audience to take a pledge and not eat out for one month. How damaging to the restaurant industry this was is a matter of mathematics.

Oprah's audience for this time frame averaged more than four million viewers, but let's call it only four million just to be on the safe side. If only half of her audience made the pledge to not eat out and only half of them actually followed this advice, we are looking at one million members of Oprah's audience staying home for thirty days. Many of these audience members have families, but let's keep the kids out of the picture and only include spouses and/or mates. So we have two million people, audience members and their spouses/mates, not eating out for one month.

Most folks eat out three to four times a week, according to an Internet poll taken during the writing of this book, but let's use three times a week. Two people eating out three times a week for four weeks is twelve visits to the local eateries during the "Noprah" pledge. Twelve multiplied by $40, the average cost for a couple to eat out, is $480. Multiply this by one million, and you have half a billion dollars. Half a billion dollars left the restaurant industry during a half-hour talk show. What does this mean to the average restaurant owner? How many of his customers would be affected by this "advice"?

It's hard to say what effect it would have on the average restaurant. However, with the restaurant business being what it is and the nature of the horrible track record of start-up restaurants, I wouldn't be surprised if this "advice" was the tipping point for quite a few failures, especially during the recession of '09. I bet you would have never thought a mid-afternoon talk show would have a God-awful effect on your business. (By the way, I am doubtful that you will see this book on Oprah's Book Club list. Wouldn't you agree?)

My second example is even more costly. Let's go back to 1993. Colorado had just passed Amendment Two. The issue surrounded rights for homosexuals, and the media elite were circling the wagons around the Colorado ski resorts. Normally, the wagons are circled to protect what is inside. This time around, they were circled to harm what was inside. At the lead of the attack was Barbara Streisand, pushing hard to keep skiers, hikers, and convention goers from the state's beautiful mountain resorts. What did the resorts do to upset Streisand so? Well...nothing. The voters of the entire state decided on Amendment Two, and it passed. What did the amendment cover? Does it matter? The resorts did not pass the bill. The resorts, their owners, the people who work there, and the people who supply these resorts could have all voted unanimously against this bill for all we know. If you owned a small concern that relied heavily on tourists such as skiers, hikers, and convention goers, how were you responsible for this bill?

Let's say you are a homosexual living in one of Colorado's ski resort towns, and you are the proud owner of a coffee shop. Your shop will, by definition, thrive on tourists. Oh sure, you can do well with the average local population, but your bread and butter is in the tourists, like most businesses of this nature in tourist-bound areas. So what do you put first, your business or your protests? If ever there was a critically defining question surrounding the crux of this book, this is it.

Streisand wanted you to close your store because you were being discriminated against. So because you were hanged instead of being more mercifully shot, we are now going to poison you. We are going to protest your state by attacking your largest industry and in turn destroy your livelihood, namely your coffee shop. But we are doing all of this for your own good.

So how many homosexual people own businesses that are related to the resort industry in Colorado? I would assume homosexual business owners are in equal numbers with the rest of our population. In other words, I would assume homosexuals are not drawn to the resort industry in Colorado nor are they deterred from it in any greater or lesser numbers than industries or states in the balance of our country. This being said, I would assume homosexual business owners are in the 5–10 percent range. This means one in ten to one in twenty business owners in the resort industry in Colorado were attacked for their own good. In case you're wondering how the boycott turned out, I have listed an excerpt from the *New York Times* dated April 1993:

"The convention business, which is often more vulnerable to boycotts, has been hit by the cancellation of 24 large meetings scheduled through 1999. But the lost revenue, estimated at $35 million over nine years, amounts to a tiny fraction of the state's $6-billion-a-year tourism industry. Colorado tourism officials say the industry this year will surpass last year's record number of ski lift tickets sold, 10.4 million, and may reach 11 million."

V. The government yet again?

Taxes, taxes, taxes, the cry of the unemployed is heard. Who cares about paying taxes if you're unemployed? The unemployed do, even if they do not know that they do. Why, you may ask, would someone who cannot find a job care what the top-line taxpayers' effective tax rate is? And no, I'm not trying to generate sympathy from the unemployed to those in the highest tax brackets. Remember, I couldn't care less what your politics are here. The lesson to be received is simply to wrap your head around a winning strategy as an entrepreneur rather than a strategy where you feel good about being right on some extraneous social issue.

Most of our country's working class, including hourly wage earners up to and including some of the top executive ranks, do not grasp how job creation truly works. If you have been a W-2 wage earner most of your life or have been surrounded by these folks, chances are very good you either have no idea of how the process of job creation works or, worse, have a completely incorrect idea of how job creation works. So let's examine this a bit closer.

A guy goes into business, hires a bunch of people, gets some customers, and becomes rich in the process on the backs of his employees. What's so hard about that? For every one that succeeds, five will fail with bankruptcy. That's what's so hard about that.

Most businesses start on the backs of the employers first and foremost. After years—yes, I said years—of doing everything from sales and marketing to cleaning the toilets, there may finally be enough left over to hire some help. Lo and behold, there lands the first employee. Now let's stop there because this is the crux of the entire job creation phenomenon. Beyond this, additional employees are mere replicas of the first employee to the small business—meaning we have a perfect "if–then" conditional. Simply explained, *if* there is enough left over, *then* hire some help. For those living in the W-2 world, the "if" portion of this conditional only refers to what comes to them in the form of a paycheck and benefits. Few, if any, truly understand what creates the "if" portion. Since most small business owners will not share the business's P&L, balance sheet, and other financial data with their employees (nor should they), I can appreciate the tribal methods of guessing at what creates the "if" portion of this conditional.

If is a very big word for just two letters. If after the cost of goods (CoG) and services rendered are paid, and if after all of the sales, general, and administrative (SG&A) costs are paid, and if after all of the local, state, and federal taxes are paid, there lies additional funds, this is where employees come from. If any of these costs increase, what happens to the employee factory? Well at first, the company begins to retract or reduce CoG and SG&A. Since most taxes are not negotiable, the next cut begins by making the employed into the *un*employed. Simple, right? Wrong.

If this were simple, there would have been a groundswell of disapproval when then senator Barack Obama suggested that spreading the wealth around was good for everyone. Do you remember a groundswell occurring? Since most Americans work for small businesses, you would think the then senator would have been summarily dispatched. But because the "if" portion was not and is not understood by most, this statement was ignored and taxes are increasing on those earning $250K per year. Unfortunately for those Americans who work for small businesses, most small business owners make more than $250K per year, or at least their tax returns show that they do. What is not explained in the tax return is that much of that $250K is going right back into the running of the small business for the following year. What was missed critically by the senator is that the $250K is revenue, not income, but our tax system does not make that distinction and taxes small business owners as if all revenue is income. If you have never worked in the small business environment, you would not understand this. Income may be used by the owner for personal items; however, most of the revenue is used for new vehicles, equipment, facilities, etc., and, yes, you guessed it, new employees or the retention of the old ones. Let's learn further from Guinevere Nell at the Heritage Foundation. This excerpt is taken from an article written in October of 2008:

"Critically important to whether a household will be affected by Senator Obama's tax increases is how income is defined. If the tax increase applies to $250,000 or more of gross income, that is quite different than $250,000 of taxable net income. This is especially true for small-business filers, as it would subject revenue, not profit, to tax."

Now that we have a grip on the difference between how much a small business earns versus how much a small business owner earns, let's now turn back to increased taxes. As the tax rates change, the balance remaining at the end of the year changes as well. This not only reduces the available capital to the business owner—you remember, "those evil rich people"—it also reduces the available capital to the business itself. Less available money means fewer employees. The vast majority of Americans should be the greatest advocate of small business owners. Instead, they are their greatest adversaries, at least at election time. In turn, this empowers factions of government that are unfriendly to small businesses to become even more embolden to act in a manner that further damages small businesses and their owners. In the end, it is the employee who is most damaged, and ironically, it occurs at and by his own hand.

All of this, of course, is in the name of fairness. Are you sure you want to keep reading? Business ownership is a continual uphill, against-the-current, sun-in-your-eyes, and wind-at-your-brow experience. The rewards, however, are immensely gratifying, and I think you know that. So on to the next section.

VI. The European Standard.

For many Americans, especially those in the media and political environments, the ultimate in working experiences is to be found in the countries of the European Union. We hear stories of starting work in the midmorning hours, taking two- to three-hour lunches, consuming alcohol during work hours, not to mention six weeks of vacation starting your first year of employment. Clearly a worker bee paradise. Or is it? Before defending against accusations that the standards you project upon your employees are harsh or cruel, let's examine a bit closer the WHOLE lifestyle of the European worker bee.

I'll give you the vacation days. Very few, if any, countries compete with Europe's vacation schedule. Ten to twelve weeks of vacation every year is not unheard of in many European nations. I'll even give you the long lunch. However, the total hours worked in a forty-hour workweek is still forty hours. Long lunches just prolong the day in my opinion, but this is a preference and clearly not truly an advantage over U.S. workers. The late start is nothing more to me than a second-shift starting early and again not an advantage.

There are other advantages born of their respective governments rather than of the employers, so we cannot compare these as apples to apples. So what do they have other than longer vacations? Well, not much. How much are you willing to give up as a U.S. worker in order to gain the additional four weeks of vacation each year? Let's take a look at the average European lifestyle versus the average American lifestyle.

The following is from a study done by a pair of economists—Fredrik Bergstrom and Robert

Gidehag—for the Swedish think tank Timbro in 2004 and reprinted in the *Wall Street Journal* in June of that same year:

"...U.S. GDP per capita was a whopping 32% higher than the EU average in 2000, and the gap hasn't closed since. It is so wide that if the U.S. economy had frozen in place at 2000 levels while Europe grew, the Continent would still require years to catch up. Higher GDP per capita allows the average American to spend about $9700 more on consumption every year than the average European. So Yanks have by far more cars, TVs, computers and other modern goods. Most Americans have a standard of living which the majority of Europeans will never come anywhere near. In the U.S. a large 45.9% of the 'poor' own their homes, 72.8% have a car and almost 77% have air conditioning, which remains a luxury in most of Western Europe. The average living space for poor American households is 1200 square feet. In Europe, the average space for *all households*, not just the poor, is 1000 square feet."

So to recap, you are free to offer your employees that extra month of vacation. In return, just ask them to give up the extra TV or the extra bedroom or the AC. I'm sure you will get an immediate no on that last one, especially if you live in the southern portion of the U.S.

Europe is what it is, and it has done what it has done, and in the end, the results are as they were originally designed. If Europe's leanings and predicaments are the predictable, then the U.S. following this lead would be the unnecessary. Once fully educated, most working people, given the opportunity, would pass on the European lifestyle in favor of the extra gadgets, living space, and disposable income. This is what makes Americans American for God's sake. The argument that the European worker has it so much better than his American counterpart is simply not factual. The AVERAGE American spends $9,700 more on consumption every year than his European counterpart. Four extra weeks of vacation would be nice, but the $9,700 represents a lot more than a trip to the shore and a stay at the European HoJo.

VII. Hard sliders are tough to hit

In very few instances are total revenues discussed, especially in the media—a dirty little secret of the tax system. Tax rates for the rich, tax rates for the poor, changes to rates, etc. are discussed ad nauseam, but rarely is the total dollars the government collects ever discussed. This is the bottom line. This is how much money the government takes from all of us—or at least those of us who are still paying taxes. So let me ask you a question. If you were the government and your intent was to pay as many of the government's bills as possible, would you be more concerned with percentages, or would you be more concerned with gross income?

If you find satisfaction in "sticking it to tha' man," then I would assume forcing the very wealthy to pay higher percentages would make you feel better, but there are two problems with that idea. First is that making the wealthy "hurt" is not going to work because income taxes are taxes on income, not net worth, so while the rich may feel a pinch on their income, their net fortunes have not been touched, not even scratched. Second, you may have gone to great lengths to make "tha' man" hurt a little, but you will have probably taken your eye off the prize. Putting your efforts into hurting "tha' man" have taken your efforts away from maximizing your gross income as a taxing entity. And the government does this all the time.

Since the dawn of income tax in 1913 (its official birth), the top-line income generators in this country have not paid the marginal rate they have been levied. In short, the richest people have always been able to pay considerably less than the percentage they are supposed to pay. For more information on this, let's visit with Arthur Laffer and an excerpt from his book *The End of Prosperity* (coauthored by Stephen Moore and Peter Tanous):

"Without getting into a long debate, let's instead look at the IRS data on income over the past thirty years. The top 1 percent of taxpayers has more than doubled from 9 percent in 1980 to 21 percent today. The share of the income to the bottom 50 percent of taxpayers has fallen from roughly 18 to 13 percent. So income distribution is becoming more skewed. The rich are indeed becoming a lot richer. The reality of less equal distribution of income is hard to deny, and we don't deny it. This is happening not just in the United States but around the globe."

Laffer et al. continues, "But here is the crucial point: The increasingly unequal distribution of income during the era of supply-side economics was the result of many millions of Americans' becoming fantastically, unthinkably rich, not a result of the poor getting poorer. In fact the vast, vast majority of the people who got rich over the last twenty-five years were not rich at the start of this period, and a good number of these people were lower middle class or poor. America cleared away the speed bumps on the path to prosperity and became an economic opportunity society. Enterprising people in huge numbers took advantage of the opportunity to amass fortunes. That's the American way."

Raising taxes on "tha' man" has done very little. In the end, the greatest damage done was to those in the top 25 percent brackets. See the chart below showing the ACTUAL tax rates paid by the top 1 percent, top 5 percent, top 10 percent, top 25 percent, and bottom 50 percent of all incomes.

	1980	2005
Top 1%	8.5%	21.0%
Top 5%	21.0%	33.0%
Top 10%	32.1%	44.4%
Top 25%	56.7%	66.1%
Bottom 50%	17.7%	13.4%

As you can see, the wealthiest of Americans are still paying less than 22 percent marginal rates. They have found a way to keep 78 percent of their income even though they should have been giving away more than 40 percent, leaving less than 60 percent and at times much less than 50 percent in their pockets.

Of more importance, I feel, is the comment made concerning the growing number of wealthy during the 1980s and early 1990s. If you just listen to the media concerning the growing number of wealthy in this time period, you are led to believe that the "divide" between the rich and the poor has the rich becoming richer and the poor becoming poorer. Nothing can be farther from the truth. The rich are getting richer, but this country's poor are not getting any poorer. They may stay the same—and there is a vast divide between American poor and what the rest of the world calls poor—or they may improve, but the trials and tribulations of one have little to do with the other.

I will leave you with this final thought from online source Wikipedia:

"In 1924, Secretary of Treasury Andrew Mellon wrote, 'It seems difficult for some to understand that high rates of taxation do not necessarily mean large revenue to the Government, and that more revenue may often be obtained by lower rates.' Exercising his understanding that '73% of nothing is nothing' he pushed for the reduction of the top income tax bracket from 73% to an eventual 24% (as well as tax breaks for lower brackets). Personal income-tax receipts rose from $719 million in 1921 to over $1 billion in 1929, which supporters attribute to the rate cut.

"Between 1979 and 2002, more than 40 other countries, including the UK, Belgium, Denmark, Finland, France, Germany, Norway, and Sweden cut their top rates of personal income tax. In an article about this, Alan Reynolds, a senior fellow with the Cato Institute, wrote, 'Why did so many other countries so dramatically reduce marginal tax rates? Perhaps they were influenced by new economic analysis and evidence from...supply-side economics.'"

Chapter 4

Internal Threats in a Bad Economy

I. The sky is falling. Where's my concrete umbrella?

This way, we get clobbered twice.
Overemphasizing caution is probably the worst stance
we can adopt in difficult times. Reactionary thinking
is not thinking. It is merely a muscle movement no
different than jerking your hand from a hot stove.
The movement need only be enough to remove the
hand from the stove, and instead, I have seen people
nearly bruise their own faces or those of the poor
souls standing within arm's reach. Entrepreneurs in
much the same manner tend to overcompensate
for the burn they feel or, even worse, the burn they
anticipate.

Of course, we can blame an overanxious and
shrieking media for much of the foolish decisions
entrepreneurs make, but I am not going to do that
in this section of the book. When it comes to poor
economies, we can almost set our watches to their
rhythms. We know, regardless of who is in political
power at the time, sooner rather than later, we will
enter a recession. Making excuses for a business

owner not seeing the next downturn is much like making excuses for a bear not fattening up during the summer. This is what we do for a living, and simply stated, there are no excuses for not being prepared when, or at the very least informed that, a recession is coming. Just like droughts following heavy rains, so too will poor economic times follow bull markets. Bet on it, bank on it, build on it.

The mass media can make whatever wild claims they wish and produce horrible stampedes in every direction possible. Yes, we can lay blame for adding fuel and fanning flames, but that fire is indigenous to the animal that is our economy. Wildfires will rage; deadwood will be devoured; and the media will tell us all about it and in the worst possible light. You, however, will stand and not waver. I quote Rostand's *Cyrano de Bergerac*: "So, when I win some triumph, by some chance, render no share to Caesar—in a word, I am too proud to be a parasite, and if nature wants the germ that grows towering to heaven like the mountain pine, or like the Oak, sheltering multitudes—I stand, not high it may be, but alone!"

And believe me, if you feel lonely running a business when the economy is clicking, I can assure you that you will feel as though you are the earth's last beating heart when the economy is clunking. Your mission, therefore, is not to ignore the rants and raves of the Woodwards but rather to adjust your sails toward the windward.

You are running a business, and businesses are large animals. When was the last time you saw a large animal retreat with the speed of a squirrel? Big animals slowly pull in their horns; big animals slowly back away; big animals slowly take up new lesser ground. I know of few businesses that are squirrels in stature. Let's go to the example box and see what we can find.

Here's an oldie but a goodie. I have changed some of the circumstances in order to protect friends and colleagues, but the gist of the story still holds much power in leading by example. The time frame was the mid to late 1980s, and Tom, Dick, and Harry were chugging along as owners of a very successful defense contractor manufacturing establishment. Their products were aiding in the battle of the Cold War, and President Reagan had the former USSR on the ropes. As you all know, the wall came down; President Reagan finished his term; and President Bush (the elder) took office. Tom, Dick, and Harry were counting on another four years of strong governmental support of their business in continued defense spending. However, one of President Bush's early agenda items was to cut defense spending. Tom and Harry began to make large motions towards selling their business, but Dick had the wherewithal to stand fast. He had a wait-and-see outlook on the new administration. The cutting was severe at first but waned with time, and the business would survive, if not thrive, through Bush's term. What loomed on the horizon was far more sinister. Tom, Dick, and Harry feared the next four years with even more trepidation. All three were sure that Clinton's administration would be the death of them, if not their business.

Try to remember, Tom and Harry had little to cheer about. The new president and both seats of Congress were Democratic and not only threatening to raise the taxes that Reagan had lowered but also aiming at destroying the defenses of this country. With all three members of government in unison, little could be done. Surely Dick would have to relent and the business would be sold.

Once again, Dick became the voice of reason and tapped the brakes instead of pressing his leg through the floorboards. He wanted to wait and see. Tom and Harry were beside themselves.

Much to Tom and Harry's amazement (not to mention the majority of the Democratic Party), the new president began to govern from the center. A quick two years and both the House and Senate did an about-face and became strong Republican majorities. Now neither party could really accomplish much of anything too terribly bad. The best thing that can happen to the business world, Wall Street, and the economy in general is the government simply going away. Writing laws that will never actually be signed into law is the next best thing, and this is what Clinton and the Republicans were facing—at least for the foreseeable future.

What if Tom and Harry had succeeded in convincing Dick to sell? Well, the actual numbers are quite staggering. If sold the first time the business was threatened, during President Bush's administration, the business would have sold for $4 million as this was the best offer at the time. If sold during the second threat, President Clinton's first two years, the business would have sold for $5 million, their top offer at that time. The business finally did sell.

On October 14, 2003, Tom, Dick, and Harry signed the documents relinquishing their business to a private equity group for $27 million. The moral of the story here is to maintain careful and watchful movements. If the sky is falling, by all means find a cave. But word that the sky is falling is simply not enough. As a business owner, you will need proof. Simply stated, in order to be successful running a small business sometimes you need to be a Dick. And no, this is not a sexist remark as some of the biggest Dicks I have ever met were women. Try taking that one out of context.

II. Quiet Desperation.

When the economy is in contraction, it may feel as though growth is nearly impossible. However, let's look at the term *growth* and more clearly define this term when the economy is down.

Think of this in terms of a long race. You're driving your race car around and around the track. Occasionally, you pass another car, and occasionally, you are the one being passed, but otherwise, the race is running along at full throttle. Then the sky begins to darken. Clouds gray the sky, and a fine mist begins to fall. The racetrack that once offered a tight grip for your tires now gives way to a slick surface. Trusted cornering and acceleration are now methods of contention as you are expending double efforts to simply complete lap after lap at only 70 percent of your former top speeds. Welcome to the race version of a down economy. We'll just call it a "wet track."

Wet-track racing requires additional attention to detail just like running a business in a down economy. Every move is slower and takes longer to accomplish. Where a foolish move on a dry track can be compensated for with a swift course correction, a misstep on a wet track will spell disaster regardless of your abilities. The result is slower, smaller movements both on the track as well as at the helm of your business. The difference between the two is that a race may actually be delayed or cancelled due to rain. Your business must run in all weather conditions and/or economic conditions.

The end result in many cases is the slower, smaller movements become minute movements soon to be no movement at all. We become paralyzed by the fear of skidding off the track and begin to run our businesses as if we had to push our cars around the track instead of using the engines. Large violent movements can and often do cause horrible accidents during slow economies, but sitting in the pits waiting for fair weather is not an option either. One must continue to strive for growth whenever possible during poor economies, especially during slow economies. There is so much more to be gained by growing during downturns in the economy. Growth during these periods is far more important than growth in strong economies.

Let's go back to the track. Let's assume you are in a strong economy, or in a dry-track race. Things are going well in your business and businesses overall, hence the strong economy. Your business is growing as are the businesses of your competitors on the track. This would be analogous to all of the race cars beginning to travel faster than they had in prior laps. Consequently, the lap times are becoming shorter and shorter, analogous to the businesses growing larger. Your speeds are exceeding 200 mph, and all is well. The very fastest cars travel 203 mph, and the very slowest travel 197 mph. Each mile per hour is another customer, another unit of profit, another unit to the top line, or whatever you wish to imagine.

Now the clouds come and the race field begins to slow more and more due to the wet track. You struggle to maintain speed but just cannot control your race car, so you too must ease off the accelerator and slow down. The field as a whole is now traveling an average of 100 mph. The fastest drivers navigate the field at 110 mph, while the slowest are driving a mere 90 mph. Did you pick up on the difference?

During strong economic times, the spread between the fastest business and the slowest is very little, a barely noticeable 6 mph. However, during the downturns, the spread is a whopping 20 mph. The spread is now noticeable and significant. Those businesses incapable of maintaining 95 mph are soon lost to the wrecker and are out of business. Those capable of running 110 mph begin to lap the remainder of the field much more quickly in a down economy than in a strong economy. If you're driving such a company, your most fervent wish is that the race officials will not call the race due to rain but rather keep running. You actually have more opportunity to gain larger ground in shorter periods of time on your competition during wet economies than dry economies. What will your business look like when the clouds retreat and the sun returns? How many laps will you be ahead of the competition when you return to fair-weather racing?

The key points here are simply these: When the clouds begin to pour in, all businesses will slow. Your aim is to slow as little as possible while still maintaining control of your business. The question to continually ask yourself as you navigate the wet track is not whether you are driving your business too fast in risky weather but rather whether you are driving your business faster than your competition. If you outpace the competition in slow periods, you are GROWING. If you are lagging behind them, you are NOT GROWING or you are experiencing negative growth. During poor economies, growth rates, either positive or negative, are accelerated and accentuated by the economy more so than during strong economies as compared to your competition. In short, your business can actually grow in comparison to your competition when in fact the overall size of your business has shrunk. Hence this is our new definition of *growth* in a down economy. Einstein said it best when he said that everything is relative.

Now that we have this in mind, you can easily see why it is so very important to do all you can to maintain your business's best posture in order to abate as much contraction as possible or, using the example above, maintain as much speed as possible while still maintaining control. Shrinking into a state of paralyzed fear will not get you around the track.

Chapter 5

Internal Threats in All Economies

I. The Presidential Campaign.

No, I am not going political on you, but I am going to use a political example to illustrate a point concerning your business. Neil and Bob are two candidates running for the White House. Horrible scandals on both candidates develop during the last two weeks of their respective campaigns. Bob meets with his campaign manager and expresses his concerns: "We need to lower our exposure in the media as much as possible." His campaign manager replies, "Bob, you committed a major crime last month. It is not going to be easy to remove this from the lead story with the media." Bob retorts, "I don't need you to remove the story. I just need you to make it smaller than the story the media has on Neil."

When you are measuring your business against competition, it is not necessary to become the greatest the world has ever seen. In the '90s, the expression was "world class," meaning you were the best that the world had to offer. There may be others as good as you, but none are better than you. I asked the question twenty years ago, and I ask the question again: why and by whose measurement?

Here's a better question: are you better than your competition? If you're running a plumbing company, why in God's name do you care if your telephone system is exceeding customer expectations? Your customers' expectations are to have their pipes fixed fast and cheap. You don't need fancy music to play while your customer sits on hold. Here's a better idea: make it so your customer doesn't sit on hold forever, and you won't need music to entertain him.

In the early '80s, manufacturing began to develop something called TQM, better known as total quality management. This involved quality circles, which were teams of employees that would meet to discuss improvements that could be made and areas where the company was lacking. In short, it was placing an emphasis on putting the customer first. I gotta ask, where the hell was the customer for the preceding hundred years?

Then in the late '80s, the government created the Malcolm Baldrige National Quality Award (MBNQA). As described by Dr. Green of Radford University, "Winning the Malcolm Baldrige National Quality Award has become a goal that many businesses strive to obtain. The award demands instant respect and admiration from others in their respective industries. Organizations that have been able to achieve this honor often find themselves turned into miniature tourist attractions for those interested in business. Individuals from around the world flock to these companies in order to obtain valuable knowledge and insight."

This was and is a wonderful award if and only if your company wins the award by doing business as it would normally have done if it had not applied to win the award. Yes, you see, you need to apply in order to be considered. So someone in your organization needs to make a conscious effort, a premeditated (you will see later why I choose this word) decision to enter his company in this competition. Within these last lines lies the problem with the Baldrige award. Company owners, directors, executives, etc. need to voluntarily stand up and crow about their organizations. Shouldn't they be more interested in running their businesses?

I will openly admit that most of the virtues of the Baldrige award are worthy and should be pursued by most companies. But not all criteria will be beneficial to all companies. If every company would benefit from every one of the seven criteria and their subsequent subcriteria of the Baldrige award, we would have a formula for success that every company on the face of the planet would be climbing over themselves to acquire and master.

Let's look at a couple of examples where the Baldrige award didn't quite work out. From the pages of the NIST (National Institute of Standards and Technology) Web site:

> "Wallace Co., Inc., a Houston-based industrial distribution company, bucked the conventional business wisdom during the mid-1980s. With the Gulf Coast economy in the doldrums and new construction activity – its primary source of revenues – at a standstill, Wallace avoided short-term remedies, and pursued a long-term strategy of Continuous Quality Improvement.
>
> "In only a few years, Wallace has distinguished itself from its competitors by setting new standards for service. It

has emerged as a stronger firm with a rapidly growing sales volume, steadily increasing market share, and better profit performance.

"Now entering the final stage of the three-phase quality program it initiated in 1985, Wallace has effectively merged business and quality goals, built new partnerships with customers and suppliers, and instilled associates with a commitment to one overriding aim: total customer satisfaction."

Now from *Business Week*:

"In 1990, the Wallace Company won the Small Business MBNQA. By October 1991 Wallace was in serious financial trouble.

"While Wallace now may be a known quantity among quality experts, it finds itself struggling against a tide of red ink. It hired a management consultant who has laid off more than one-fourth of the 280 employees and is trying to ward off hungry creditors. If the company can't persuade them to reschedule $17 million in debt, this Baldrige winner could wind up in bankruptcy before October is out." (Ivey and Carey 1991)

How could this happen to an MBNQA winner? Wallace had spent much money on quality-related improvements such as computers and changes in their processes. Company overhead increased by $2 million a year. With customers balking at price hikes, an industry-wide recession helped place Wallace in a weak financial position. Wallace was receiving up to eighty requests per day for information about the award and daily plant tours. Company executives were flying around the country making speeches about their quality journey and successes. As CEO John W. Wallace said, "We were so busy doing the presentations that we weren't following up and getting the sales" (Ivey and Carey 1991).

Wallace had become a sideshow instead of a business. Their goals had been defined by an award instead of by simple measurements of success. They didn't need to be the best to be incredibly successful and outpace their competition, but they did in order to win the shiny award, an award that decorated a bookshelf. I would guess it was placed somewhere between Chapters 9 and 13.

Need another example? Well, let's move eastward to a larger company. Ever heard of Eastman Chemical Company? Eastman won the Baldrige award in 1993. Shortly thereafter they began to run into financial troubles.

Need more? Let's look at Motorola and Xerox. Merrill Lynch is also on that list. All of these companies have landed in serious trouble over the past few years shortly after winning the Baldrige award.

My point here is not that the Baldrige award is the kiss of death. Far from it. The award in its purest form provides accolades to companies that are excelling in their fields. They are indeed probably "world-class" organizations, and they deserve all of the credits they have had bestowed upon them. The question I have is, "Why did they apply to be considered for this award in the first place?"

This award is sought much like the Holy Grail. Men who seek this prize must ask themselves, "Do you seek the Grail for your glory or His?" Is this award for personal bragging rights or as a by-product of your organization's hard work? One of the best responses I have ever heard came from Earnest Deavenport, former chairman and chief executive officer of Eastman Chemical Company. He said, "Eastman, like other Baldrige award winners, didn't apply the concepts of total quality management to win an award. We did it to win customers. We did it to grow. We did it to prosper and to remain competitive in a world marketplace."

The point of the award for Mr. Deavenport was purely marketing. That I can relate to and admire. Taking your eye off the prize, operating a well-run and profitable business, in order to take home a piece of acrylic with your name etched on it just doesn't make any sense. Now for the reality check.

Most of you have not applied and may not ever apply for a Baldrige award. However, what other distractions are you giving your time and attention to that are just as potentially destructive as, if not more so than, some award? You need only be the less distasteful presidential candidate. Give that your time and attention.

II. Are you kidding me? We're gonna sell millions.

This is one of the main reasons businesses fail due to ownership. Picture this. You are having lunch with a friend who is about to launch a new business. He is describing in great detail the new office, potential employees, storefront, marketing campaign, financing being finalized, etc., when you stop him and ask what it is he will be selling. You then ask, "So what method of marketing did you use to research how many units you are going to be able to sell?" His response is, "Marketing method? Are you kidding me? We're gonna sell millions."

This is either an accident waiting for a victim or an unexplainable success happening in spite of ownership. Both fly in the face of logic. I share a story of Bertrand Russell, the late Nobel Prize winner and master logician. Russell, as the story was told to me, once said, "Grant me one false assumption, and I can prove anything."

A listener then responded by challenging Russell, "Okay, assuming one plus one equals one, prove to me that you and the pope are the same."

Russell's response: "I'm one. The pope is one. One plus one equals one. So we are the same."

The point of the story is that if a logical argument relies on just one false assumption, the whole argument fails. Many people use this principle to persuade others into believing things that are wrong. It's simply a matter of putting a few false assumptions at the beginning of your argument, making what follows seem logical, and hoping no one will notice. *Assuming* large sales rather than investigating true market potential is all that is needed to convince someone of the *guaranteed* success of a new business.

The most important question a new business venture must ask itself is, "Is there a market for me?" The largest percentage of small business failures occur due to insufficient market support. The business owners who are most guilty of this offense are those who strongly feel they are right and that being right is more important than having a business that is successful.

Far too many entrepreneurs rely solely on their gut feelings when starting their businesses with little to no verification of actual demand. And so many times actual demand is counterintuitive to what you might believe to be true. A good example is the sale of sunglasses in Seattle, Washington. If you were a salesman for my sunglasses company and I told you that your sales territory was going to be the Pacific Northwest, I would imagine you would be disappointed. After all, Seattle and the surrounding territories are not known for bright sunshine. On the contrary, steady and heavy rains accompanied by days of overcast clouds are more of what most think to be the weather conditions in that part of the country. But what happens when the sun finally does break through those clouds?

If you have been accustomed to day-in, day-out clouds and rain, how well adapted are your eyes to bright sunlight? The first thing you are going to reach for is your shades. Consequently, sunglasses sales in the Seattle area are quite strong. Who woulda thunk it?

Now, how many counterintuitive business plans can you dream up that are failures waiting to happen? Only market research will tell you if your town really needs a lube center, another dry cleaner, a sales agency, a public relations firm, or a sunglasses retailer.

Market research does not need to be high-level, Twelfth Avenue–type research. It can simply be going out and talking to existing businesses in related industries, suppliers to these industries, your chamber of commerce, trade associations, or at the very least, potential customers. Your goal is to get a real-world view of your target audience and make sure that first and foremost the audience is in fact "millions." You cannot sell millions if your audience is only dozens. Then try to collect as much feedback on existing products or services as you can to give yours the best possible chance of landing the millions that are out there.

Please remember, your product or service may be the best ever. Your gut instincts may indeed be correct, and everyone should beat a path to your door. However, your product may also be too ahead of its time, or the market may already be overstocked and oversupplied with Brand Z. Stock traders' first rule is to not fall in love with a stock. Your first rule is to not fall in love with your product or service. A cunning entrepreneur knows when to cut his losses and move on. A pompous intellectual knows what he knows, and his nose knows not where it should not insert itself. Please excuse the double negative.

Let's get back to your friend and lunch. So you're about done eating, and your friend finally shuts up and asks you what you think of him trying to open a retail chainsaw store on U.C. Berkley's campus. You slowly hand him the bill for your food and tell him you will take care of the tip. Then you lean in slightly and scream, "Are you kidding me? You cannot create demand!" Then you quietly ask him if his business plan has scheduled a bailout.

III. Stop apologizing. Bigger is bigger, but smaller is vital.

So many small business owners walk around like they have done something wrong by being successful, and so many new business owners don't fully grasp how vital they are in their communities and in society as a whole. I will get to the former later and the latter first.

How vital are small businesses? Well, according to the Small Business Administration's Office of Advocacy, here are some key statistics. Small businesses (and I quote):

- "represent 99.7 percent of all employer firms";
- "employ about half of all private sector employees";
- "pay nearly 45 percent of total U.S. private payroll";
- "have generated 60 to 80 percent of net new jobs annually over the last decade";
- "create more than half of the nonfarm private gross domestic product (GDP)";
- "hire 40 percent of high tech workers (such as scientists, engineers, and computer workers)";
- "are 52 percent home-based and 2 percent franchises";
- "made up 97.3 percent of all identified exporters and produced 28.9 percent of the known export value in FY 2006";
- "produce 13 times more patents per employee than large patenting firms; these patents are twice as likely as large firms to be among the one percent most cited."

From Texas Wesleyan University we learn these tidbits:

- "89% of incomes over $50,000 a year are earned by owners of small businesses."
- "4 out of 5 businesses don't last 5 years and few ever earn the profits they should."

Getting back to the SBA and being more specific, since the mid-1990s, "small businesses have created 60 to 80 percent of the net new jobs. Using data from 2005, small businesses have created 979,102 net new jobs, or 78.9 percent. Meanwhile, large firms added 262,326 net new jobs or 21.1 percent. Small businesses employ about half of U.S. workers. Of 116.3 million nonfarm private sector workers in 2005, small firms employed 58.6 million and large firms employed 57.7 million. Firms with fewer than 20 employees employed 21.3 million." It turns out that your tiny little candy store employs one in five Americans in the private sector. Consequently, you are providing the working wages for 20 percent of this country's people in the private sector. Now how vital is that? Well...pretty damn vital. But let's not stop there.

Continuing from the SBA, "In 2007, there were 27.2 million businesses in the United States, according to Office of Advocacy estimates. Small firms represent 99.9 percent of the 27.2 million businesses (including both employers and nonemployers), as the most recent data show there were slightly more than 17,000 large businesses in 2005." Or as I like to restate this figure, small businesses outnumber large businesses 1,598.4 to 1.

I believe being a successful small business owner is nothing to feel guilty about; on the contrary, it is something you should be shouting from the rooftops. Again from the SBA, U.S. Department of Commerce, Bureau of the Census, U.S. Department of Labor, and the Employment and Training Administration, the following table illustrates just how difficult it is to be a successful small business owner:

Category	2003	2004	2005	2006	2007
New Firms	612,296	628,917	644,122	640,800	637,100
Closures	540,658	541,047	565,745	587,800	560,300
Bankruptcies	35,037	34,317	39,201	19,695	28,322

For those of you who would like the above broken down into a single sentence: "66 percent of new employer establishments survive at least two years, 44 percent survive at least four years, and 31 percent survive at least seven years," according to a study by the SBA. The odds of survival are better on the Serengeti.

If you can make it past the odds and actually survive the first seven years, you do indeed have a rare commodity, a successful small business. Of course, you then need to somehow overcome the skyrocketing cost of employee benefits, double taxation, and employee regulations (which are 45 percent more expensive for small businesses than for large businesses due to economies of scale), and in the end, the few drops of profits left in the till are yours. Of course, those profits may have a hard time finding their way into your pocket when they are being spread around to make things more "plumb" for those who didn't even try to do any of what you did.

So stop walking around like your successful business or your intent to have a successful business is akin to eating a cheeseburger while on a diet. In my opinion, you have earned the right to order the entire left side of the menu at your local burger joint. Just don't mega-size it. No one likes a greedy success story.

IV. Gimme an A. Gimme a B. Give me three Ds: death, divorce, and disability.

This is an internal threat where the true know-it-all insists on being right or the true procrastinator insists on being lazy. In either case, the business owner, after all the hard work and long hours are spent building the entity to a place where it is actually worth something, loses everything to a spouse, heirs, a partner, or the government.

i. Let's start with death.

This is a simple one since we all have this issue coming one way or another. If there is only one owner, what could possibly be the concern? The owner dies, and the family inherits the business. What's the problem? Ask the Robbie family.

The following is from an online informational Web site, Findmyinsurance.com, writer unknown:

> Joe Robbie was an American success story. He was a successful entrepreneur and co-founder of the Miami Dolphins, a franchise that turned into one of the highest profile and most lucrative teams in professional football. During his span as owner, Robbie and Coach Don Shula led the Dolphins to an unfathomable 14-0 perfect season, won two Super Bowls (1973 and 1974) and built $115 million Joe Robbie Stadium. At the time, unlike any other open-air facility, Joe Robbie Stadium was the first to be constructed entirely with private funds. [Something not even Jerry Jones of the Dallas Cowboys was able to achieve in today's multibillion-dollar NFL market. Just ask any Arlington, Texas, taxpayer.]
> Like many owners of family-run businesses, it was Robbie's dream to have his family follow in his footsteps when he was gone.

Unfortunately, Robbie never planned to deal with estate taxes. He died on January 7, 1990. Through the marriage deduction, he passed to his wife the illustrious franchise and the stadium which bore his name. Unfortunately, his wife passed away soon thereafter, and due to a lack of planning, a staggering estate bill estimated at $47 million was left behind. Differing views amongst his nine children only exacerbated the situation and forced the cash-poor family to sell Robbie's legacy he had worked so hard to build. In 1994, the family sold both the team and the stadium for a total of $138 million. At that time, the sale price, even after estate taxes, was impressive. Today, many would argue that the Dolphins and the stadium – now known as Pro Player Stadium – might be worth twice as much. More important, however, Robbie's intentions were defeated; his family was removed from the success he worked so hard to build.

The Robbie story is atypical since the surviving spouse is usually around long enough to pass on the business to the next generation. What is more tragic is when there is more than one business owner—the partnership. Equal partnership among two or more partners is a recipe for disaster when one of the partners dies. Why should this be a problem if all that needs to be done is giving the surviving spouse his share of the value of the business? But what if the surviving partner does not want cash but rather wants to take the deceased partner's place in the firm? What happens when you have a "new" partner who is a mental train wreck? Or worse yet, what happens if the surviving spouse wants the cash, and your organization is not liquid enough to write the check?

Can you see how many different scenarios can spell disaster—or should I say spell bankruptcy— for the business and your life after the death of a partner? Preparation with simple estate planning can stiff-arm this potential problem. Make sure you speak with an estate planner who specializes in small business estate planning. Don't milk a cow and expect ice cream. All estate planners are not the same.

ii. Now to one of my favorites, divorce.

Not a favorite because I enjoy the concept of a marriage ending but because this is the only one of the Ds where someone actually is making a decision to destroy the business. The ending of the business may not be the sole intent of the divorcing spouse, but make no mistake, it is in fact one of the considerations in the decision process. In other words, someone is knowingly destroying the business or, at the very least, making an attempt to find the business's limits of endurance.

Here's the story. Two partners own ABC Camera and Supply. In ten years, the photographer's retail supplier has grown to three locations and is now doing $6 million in sales annually. All of a sudden, one of the spouses decides she wants out. The soon-to-be-divorced partner grants the divorce, which includes the house, a car, the kids, etc. Unfortunately, the business does not have $1.5 million in cash (25 percent of $6 million in gross sales, which is an estimate that may in fact be too conservative depending on the valuation method at the time of the divorce) to give her to settle the divorce.

No problem, she will just help run the business as a 25 percent partner. Can you imagine this frontal lobotomy of a business? Not only does the divorcé now share his business with his ex-wife, whom he probably hates with the white-hot intensity of a thousand suns, but he has also lost his fifty-fifty partnership authority to his business partner. See, the business partner still has the other 50 percent of the business, and the divorcé's 50 percent has now been split in half. To me, this would be like being shot and then hung. Or is it hanged?

Let's look at the other way this one could have gone. The business doesn't have the $1.5 million in cash. Her attorney says, "Tough. Get it any way you can." The only solution is to sell the business or declare bankruptcy—two options that are kind of like the difference between hospital food and airplane food. The good news is that the sleepless nights the divorcé's about to have will give him a chance to catch up on the latest infomercials. (My favorite is the mandolin vegetable slicer that can also be used to strip the waxy buildup on your hardwood floors.)

To avoid this problem, find a good estate planner. Agreements can be drafted that will spread equity payments over a period of years, thereby allowing the business to make payments from yearly cash flows instead of one lump sum. And this is only one suggestion. There are dozens of potential defenses to the divorce audible.

iii. Lastly, there is disability.

This one really plays into the hand of the eternal "right versus winning" mentality. Simply stated, the business owner is never going to get sick, never going to have an accident, never going to have any health issues...ever. The 27 million businesses in this country are run by HealthyMan. He flies around with a big H on his chest, going from meeting to meeting, never even once suffering from a sniffle.

Of course, I am being facetious. Can you imagine the immune system of someone in the environment of an entrepreneur? Unbelievable stress coupled with eating fast food on the run coupled with poor sleep and virtually no exercise. Did you count one thing that can be considered healthy in the business owner's life? He needs an H on his chest like a zebra needs a bicycle.

It's a wonder more small business owners just don't drop dead left and right. With the stresses most small business owners endure, we should be stepping over them at every turn. I can hear the complaints coming from teens at the mall: "Oh my God. Can we get some kind of snow plow to move these small business owners out of the food court?"

Thinking your body can endure this kind of stress year in and year out is just not practical. Sooner or later, something is going to give out. I'll give you an example. I looked through my cell phone and picked a letter. I chose H since I had been using this previously. Of the folks I have in my cell phone under H, there are four who either currently run a small business or at one time ran a small business.

Of those four, three have had a major health issue to deal with in one form or another. One had a stint implanted after a heart attack. One had a crushed pelvis from a car accident while en route to a customer meeting. And the last has come down with adult diabetes. Half of my H friends and acquaintances who have experience running a small business have had issues with a disability in either a temporary or permanent capacity.

And yes, I understand you could argue that this is not a scientific study and that real statistical analysis would need to be performed, but my point would still be true. My example included those listed under the H on my cell phone. The numbers increase under M and R. The driver here is that the human body can only take so much. The odds are against you in your keeping perfect health during your sojourn into entrepreneurship. As always, speak to an estate planner and your insurance specialist, even if you're foolish enough to wear a cape and boots—right, Lois?

V. I'm sorry, Mr. Smith; your company is bleeding equity internally. I'm afraid it is terminal.

If only there was a physician you could send your company to for a full physical. Some accountants will perform this function for you, and certainly banks can give you a good idea of the health of your organization. The downside is that they will look at your financials from the perspective of an accountant and a banker. While this can be helpful, it is not necessarily ideal.

Most bankers as well as most accountants have never run a business themselves. How many stories have you heard of a loan officer at Bank A turning down a loan to some small company and then Bank X grants the loan and the company rockets to the stratosphere? What did Bank A not see, or what did it pay too much attention to that forced it to turn its nose up at granting the loan? What was it that caused the bank to view this small company in such a negative light? Was it male ownership? Just kidding. Whatever it was, bear in mind if you take your financials to a banker to review, the feedback you receive may be biased. Does a bad report from a bank mean your organization is on the verge of needing a transfusion? If you cannot read financial statements, how would you know?

If you are unable to decipher financial statements, you are in much the same predicament as those poor souls consulting with physicians on the health of their bodies. An even more frightening example would be the helpless feeling one gets when talking to his mechanic. I'm not sure which profession is more proficient at performing a colonoscopy, metaphorical or otherwise.

In either case, you are at the mercy of someone else's expertise. A second opinion is always an option, but going from one banker to another or one accountant to another may not reveal any additional information or give the true health of the organization. I once asked my CPA for her professional opinion on the financial strength of a company I owned. Her response was, "You're doing well." What the hell does that mean? In today's litigious environment, I would assume this to be a pat answer and yet another roadblock to truly understanding the health of the business.

The problem is that bankers and accountants are trained to look for elements in financial statements that are important to *them and their job responsibilities*. That training does not prepare them to give advice to business owners with suggestions concerning the potential overreliance on inventory, carrying too little cash, carrying too much cash, when to reduce overhead, and so on. Indicators such as these come from two things: instruction from an individual on the fundamentals of reading a financial statement and the consequential business experience that follows.

How do you gain experience to help prevent you from failing in business if you fail at running your business? Good question. Ask for some guidance from other business owners. This is where networking helps. No, I am not suggesting that you become a social butterfly, but consulting two or three other business owners who have some experience under their belts would be just what the doctor ordered. Just remember what a very successful entrepreneur once shared with me: "Never take advice from someone who is not doing *much* better than you are."

If you take that statement to heart, few are qualified to give you advice, period. Especially as your business grows, fewer and fewer people will be of a station greater than yours. I speak here strictly in the arena of *business* experience, but I have found this to apply to other venues of *life* experience. In any event, choose wisely when it comes to mentors.

With a good seminar or two under your belt and the kind sharing of experience from well-matured mentors, you will be on your way to understanding the key drivers of a healthy business and the kamikaze killers of a hellish business.

The scope and depth of this book is not that of a financial text. However, this topic is so vital to your success as a business owner that I am going to touch on some of the high points. The best method is to learn to read the "x-ray" yourself. The good news is that you don't need to go through four years of medical school, one year of internship, and one year of residency. No need to be a Rhodes scholar.

There are three fundamental financial statements you must fully understand:

- Profit and loss (P&L) – this is what your company did over a period of time; the capability, if you will, of your organization for a specific past period of time.
- Balance sheet – this is where your company is at a particular point in time. I emphasize "point in time" especially for seasonal businesses.
- Cash flow statement – this is the history of the sources, uses, and profits of your organization, and no, they are not all the same thing.

Every item listed on the above reports is important. Some are more important than others. The distinction among all of the items listed in financial statements is not importance but rather urgency. To continue with the medical metaphor, each step in surgery is important but not all are urgent. Keeping the temperature of the operating room rather cool is an *important* step to reduce the chance of infections. Injecting the patient with enough drugs to keep him sedated during the operation is an *urgent* step. Catch the distinction? I know I would be upset if I woke up in the middle of my operation.

Lowering your telephone bill may be important but does not need to be done this instant. However, raising enough capital to make it through the week? Well, that one would be urgent. I know this sounds simple, and I may be overstating the obvious, but you would be surprised how many business owners I have come across who spend undue time dissecting the death out of an invoice or a bank statement only to discover they spent four hours of detective work trying to find eight cents. Such behavior is oh so very foolish. Please let me prove it to you.

Let's suppose you are the sole employee of a business, and that business earns a top-line income of $100,000 per year. You will work roughly 2,000 hours at a minimum over the course of the year. Your hourly rate of return on the top line is $50 an hour. Spending four hours to find $0.08 is a net loss of $199.92. This behavior repeated can cast your doom.

Your financials will tell you exactly how much you are worth to your organization per hour no matter how many employees you have and regardless of income. These three statements will instruct you not only where to spend your time as the lead surgeon on your operating team but also what to spend your time doing. One-man operating teams do it all. Contrary to this, the lead surgeon performing a quadruple bypass is never seen taking blood pressure readings. Your financials will tell you what level of surgery your organization is capable of performing.

From the mundane to the monstrous, all can be found in the few pages of the financial statements. There will usually be three to four risks that you should be constantly analyzing in order to explain and evaluate them. These will be the monsters, and they will be very apparent. There will also always be the "pain in the rear" minutiae. These will be the mundane.

Both of these will rise and fall and move in and move out of focus with the passing months. Monsters are money junkies, and the mundane are time robbers. Be cautious in preventing the monsters' money from consuming too much of your time and the mundane's time from consuming too much of your money. In short, don't let your dollars wait on your dimes.

One last tidbit regarding financial statements: much like the undulations of the waves across the sea, your statements will increase and decrease. Each line item will rise and fall. When the key income drivers (sales, gross profits, income, net income, etc.) begin to fall, all other items should fall in equal percentages. If the sea is at ten feet, this means a cork floating on the sea surface has as much chance at being five feet above the mean sea elevation as it does five feet below the mean sea elevation. When the sea goes to twenty feet, now your cork is somewhere between ten above and ten feet below.

If sales drop 10 percent, your cost of goods, operating expenses, etc. should be somewhere between 10 percent down and 10 percent up. A drop of 10 percent in sales does not justify your cost of goods increasing 25 percent. This would be considered a rogue wave and is a sure sign you're facing potential trouble. Over time, you will adapt a feeling for the sea much like a seasoned skipper sailing the North Sea.

Business, like nature, has a rhythm. This makes sense since business is driven by humans, and humans are part of nature—believe it or not. If you sense something is wrong, you're probably right. Look deeper. This is where you earn that $50-per-hour top-line revenue.

VI. Monkey see, monkey do. What if the first monkey is blind?

This threat never ceases to amaze me. Companies of all sizes commit this felony of the financial disciplines. If XYZ firm decides to buy the latest computer system, or software, or new piece of heavy equipment, or high-profile advertising space, etc., then competitor ABC firm quickly follows suit in fear of XYZ gaining a quick advantage.

I fully understand the instincts our humanity handicaps us with and our need to feel that we are not falling by the wayside, especially when it comes to our competitors. However, let's remember to take a moment and consider the following three questions. We will use a new software package as a simple example.

i. Why is XYZ firm acquiring this software package?

Is it that their current package is horribly outdated? Did they acquire a customer that is demanding additional capabilities? There could be a hundred reasons for their decision, some good and some bad, that may or may not apply to your world. In other words, they may need to make this move with a new software package purely due to circumstances that do not exist in the land of ABC. And this may be a wonderful thing for you and ABC.

ii. Is XYZ worth mimicking?

I'll give you a perfect example. Let me take you back to my ninth-grade health class. It's third period, and our teacher has drawn two lines on the blackboard. Line A is about a foot long, and Line B is about five feet long. He asks for a show of hands of who believes Line A is longer than Line B. At first few, if any, hands are raised, but then nerdy Christopher raises his hand. Christopher is known among most in the class as a know-it-all and a public nose picker, but he does get good grades—and very few dates, might I add.

Anyway, Christopher raises his hand. Slowly but surely, about eight or so more hands go up. Today, we would call these students sheep. Herd animals or not, they are indeed followers. Unfortunately for the sheep that day, our teacher had pulled Christopher aside before the class began and asked him to raise his hand thereby giving a false endorsement to the wrong answer. The fix was in, and the sheep fell for it.

Now back to XYZ, and I ask the same question. Are they worth mimicking? Are they really so smart that you would want to follow them off the proverbial cliff? If they are that smart, are you smart enough to distinguish their strategies in buying software as forthright or deliberately fixed? Are they baiting you?

If the answers to these questions are favorable, then by all means follow XYZ to the ends of the earth. Just keep in mind that many of our largest institutions (banks, investment firms, insurance companies, etc.), employing some of our smartest business men and women, have followed each other through the early years of this millennium straight off a cliff—a cliff where gravity is spelled CDO. Few, if any, are truly immune to the bandwagon approach to running a business. Repeatedly ask yourself, "Will this new software really help my business, and if so, do I really need it now?"

iii. If a new software package is a really good idea, do I want the same one as XYZ?

Just because XYZ is a competitor, does this mean we automatically would benefit from the same software package, the same advertising strategies, and the same brand of coffee in the break room? Competition can vary widely in form, fit, and function. Another example may be helpful.

XYZ and ABC are both real estate agencies. Both firms list and sell high-end homes. Both firms list and sell homes in exactly the same neighborhoods. Both firms have exactly the same number of agents and exactly the same volume in terms of yearly sales dollars. You would think that the same exact marketing approach would work for both firms. Yet each time ABC Real Estate tries to move their marketing from the Internet to the local periodicals, they experience a drop in sales. And each time XYZ Real Estate tries to move their marketing from the local periodicals to the Internet, they experience a drop in sales.

How can the two be inversely related? On the surface, they appear to be identical firms. However, just below the surface, we find the difference. It appears that one firm has by default come to specialize in listing homes. The other firm has grown a niche business by selling homes. The two firms complement each other rather well and over time will probably come to realize this. For the time being, however, making any attempt to "shadow" each other's marketing approaches will spell disaster.

While a marketing plan is without a doubt a necessary strategy in the two firms' real estate market, the methodologies, strategies, and solutions are vastly different. If their marketing were a software program, one would be PC based and the other would be Mac based, and the two would not work on each other's platforms.

VII. 'Cause breaking up is hard to do...

Ever hear the story of the boss and the secretary? The boss cheats on his wife with his secretary. He then divorces his wife and marries his secretary. The boss then begins to cheat on his new wife with his new secretary. The truly sad part about this story is that the new wife is stunned that he is cheating on her with the new secretary. "If I only had a clue that he was the kind of person that would hurt me. If there was just some clue of his true nature," she is heard to utter.

We call this the chameleon syndrome. The color changes to suit the viewer's expectations.

Hiring employees can be much the same incubator of insanity. Every day, people seeking employment darken your door. And every day, everything from basket cases to out-and-out criminals are hired by firms that are completely oblivious to the true nature of their new hires or, even worse, are aware of their past poor behaviors and hire them anyway. Employees, much like children, will be your source of greatest anxiety as well as potentially the source of your greatest pride. In the upcoming examples, you will see why the thought of a child came to mind.

Many years ago, I had a temporary employee working for me named Billy. It was my policy to bring on all new hires as temporaries for sixty days—a policy I still support, by the way. Even with some of the more sophisticated screening techniques, a chameleon can still sneak by you. Hiring on a sixty-day temporary basis is a simple safeguard from having to waste human resources' time and energy on an individual who is just not going to work out. It is by far much easier on your team and the temporary to break with your relationship if he has not yet become a fully fledged member of your family.

Anyway, back to my temporary. At forty-five days, I would send all temporaries that were being considered for long-term employment with our firm to a drug-screening clinic for testing. Billy was doing exceptionally well at his job, and I really liked his attitude toward challenges and problems. He possessed a natural problem-solving ability that just cannot be taught. So off he went to be tested, and seventy-two hours later, I received the results: positive for amphetamines.

The denials came quickly. Billy was emphatic that he did not do drugs and that there must have been some kind of mix-up at the clinic. So an additional seventy-two hours and an additional $75 later, the second round of test results came back: positive for amphetamines. I can remember asking myself, "Oh what fresh hell is this?"

If I told you that I hired Billy anyway, would you believe me? Would you want to slap me? Would I want to slap myself?

Fast-forward to the arbitration for the lawsuit brought by one of my other employees after Billy showed up to work higher than a kite and decided to assault her in the parking lot. Her attorney sued everyone, especially the foolish employer who disregarded not one but TWO drug screenings that warned Billy had a high probability of showing up to work in an altered state of mind. Fifty thousand dollars later, the new policy was to pay attention to the first drug screening.

And no, this was not my hire but that of a friend of mine. I used myself as the foolish employer in this story because I followed this same path and did hire a "Billy." Fortunately for me, he began missing work due to his drug use, and I had to let him go for poor attendance. "There but for the grace of God..."

Here's another fine example of a hiring disaster. After hearing of a particularly gruesome hiring mistake, I asked the business owner of a fairly successful investment firm, "Did you do any background checks to see if she had any kind of criminal record?" The reply came in the form of a smile and a headshake side to side. "How was I supposed to know she had a criminal history? I guess it's my fault that she broke in and took ten thousand dollars' worth of our computer equipment."

My reply was a smile and a headshake up and down. "Running a successful business is difficult enough. Making a mistake hiring someone who cannot get to work on time is bad. Hiring someone with the likelihood of theft is disastrous." Hiring a "Billy" can be life altering. Any of your current employees can become a "Billy," and there isn't a screening process in the world that will predict a transformation from an ideal employee to a maniac. Would it not be prudent then to use the screening that is available? With the poor odds in mind, why not take advantage of the screening that is available? Give yourself the best possible chance to not make a ridiculous mistake. In short, don't bring a knife to a gunfight.

Fees for full physiological, drug, criminal, and financial screening can vary widely and are generally not performed by just one company. My best suggestion is to ask other business owners who they use, if they use any screeners, and get their take on performance and costs. This is such a potentially painful subject to most business owners that I have found most to be more than willing to share their experiences even with competitors. A poor hire is the kind of disaster you wouldn't wish on your worst enemy, not even your competition.

A poor hire is like a really bad-tasting cough medicine—a cough medicine that tastes so bad, you end up taking care of yourself so much better just to avoid ever having to take any of the cough medicine ever again. The winning move is to do without the additional employee rather than make a poor hiring choice. This is the classic example of addition by subtraction. Rather than walking into work with all of your best employees in an uproar due to a horrible attitude from one hiring mistake, you simply make do until a good hire becomes available. Good, tired employees are better than good, pissed-off employees.

There are countless volumes written on the hiring mistakes that are most likely to plague your organization. I am not going to delve into this area in much more depth as solutions to these issues are spelled out quite clearly in these volumes. Remember, my intent is to focus on the mind of the business owner. If I could fix problematic mental shortcomings with a simple instruction to read a book, other than this one, I would do so. Hiring mistakes caused by owners' paradigms are simple to overcome, for the most part, with short books on each respective topic. However, here are a few suggestions on hiring. Like I said, additional information on each item is easily found at the local bookstore or online.

i. Don't just chat during an interview.

If you're hiring an administrative person, give him some computer work to perform. If you're hiring a journeyman plumber, give him something to plumb. If driving a car is a daily activity, by all means get behind the wheel in bumper-to-bumper traffic and see how he performs. I can talk my way through eighteen holes and shoot five under par. Funny how the results change when I actually pick up a golf club.

ii. Don't let human resources do the recruiting.

I once saw a human resources manager toss a résumé for an engineering position because the candidate did not show experience with AutoCAD 11.

He did have solid model experience with Solidworks. For those who do not work with these engineering software packages, this is the equivalent of passing on a chef who is a graduate of the cordon bleu because he did not list the ability to make beanie-weenies.

It is a practical impossibility for human resources to be aware of all of the specifics for any given position. Department managers need to do the screening. Don't set human resources up to commit your failures. At the same time, don't allow human resources to determine who you should or should not interview. They will not take responsibility for your hiring mistakes. Conversely, don't give them the power to take away a star player because his résumé was not written to be read by the technically challenged.

iii. The passive job hunter is out there, and you may need to go find him instead of vice versa.

Don't make a hire just to fill a slot. You may want to hold a warm body as a temp for an extended period of time, but don't put a person in a position when you know he will be eventually fired or quit out of duress. Wait for the right person or go and get him. Again, this is addition by subtraction.

iv. Get your team involved.

Everyone who will interact with the new hire for more than one cumulative hour per week needs to chat with the interviewee for at least ten to fifteen minutes. Whether this is conducted one-on-one or in a group is for you to decide, but all must give their thumbs up or down, and this must be done during a one-on-one with you. This way, you remove the peer pressure your current employees may have on each other in discussing the new guy. All thumbs up does not mean you make an offer, but all thumbs down means your folks are probably trying to tell you something.

v. Lastly, if you are committing any of the above, don't try to change your hiring process in one fell swoop.

Do yourself a favor and tackle one at a time or as the new positions come up. Then stand back and take a look at the quality improvement in people as you place more and more requirements on hiring employees. One colleague compared his old employees to his new ones as being akin to the wall chart depicting the evolution of man—a comparison that I thought was a bit crude...until I attended his company picnic. If you're ever in a similar position, make sure you keep Homo Habilis away from the grill.

VIII. "How the hell are we supposed to grow if these customers keep bothering us?"

Go ahead and laugh it up, but this was an actual quote from the customer service manager at a customer of mine that was in a strong growth mode many years ago. Her solution was to actually cut back on the number of customers they serviced. I know this is hard to believe, but this is what she was actually recommending.

What's more unbelievable is the number of firms out there that do exactly the same thing. No, they don't have a fool running their customer service department, but they do, by default, limit the number of customers that can begin to use their goods and services by use of antiquated customer service methods, inadequate client relationship software, poor delivery of goods or services, etc. So many small firms fight hard for their limitations by seeing themselves as a tiny firm and believing in managing by means of entrenched maintenance.

They are deep in the trenches and appear to like it there, or at least their behavior would lead you to believe this. Maintaining the current level of customers is all they can see as the forest becomes something other than the trees, not realizing that all businesses have attrition. Each firm will lose a percentage of its clients every year, and every year, the firm will need to bring in this same percentage just to maintain the current sales levels. Entrenched maintainers many times realize this far too late, only when the firm has fallen below its critical mass and begins to take drastic steps in order to keep the lights on.

Firms with strong sales always seem to have expenses take care of themselves. Nurture the dollars, and the dimes will take care of themselves. Moreover, firms with strong sales tend to attract the attention of capital.

Bad habits like poor back-office management, inept leadership, and backward technical vision can all be fixed by new management. Poor sales, on the other hand, is a problem unto itself and can be an indicator that the business is modeled incorrectly. In short, strong sales means the body may be rotting off of the frame but the car still runs. Poor sales means the engine may or may not start. Which car would you rather have? Which car will a bank be more interested in lending money to buy?

I am not proposing growing beyond controlled limits but rather maintaining manageable growth. It is not that difficult to figure out what percentage of your current clients will not be there for you next year. Whatever the number is, this is your MINIMUM sales target for the current year. Beyond that, you have achieved what we like to call GROWTH. Below that, you are RECEDING. Exactly that is damn near impossible, so we're not even going to give it a name. Right is a slice, left is a hook, and straight is a miracle, to use the terms of a golf beginner.

I met a business owner at a recent seminar I attended. She and her husband owned a construction company that specialized in outdoor kitchens. She said every year she needed to replace 100 percent of her clients. I would assume swimming pool installation companies are also in this same boat. One hundred percent of your clients would, of course, be the worst case. The best case would be something like a medical practice where, depending on your type of practice, you would lose 2–5 percent to client relocation, changing physicians, or (God help your practice) death. Where on this scale of 2 percent to 100 percent does your firm lie?

If you see a problem with replacing clients due to attrition, you may want to reconsider your business model. I see little point in building a business only to see it collapse before your very eyes because the market could not overcome attrition.

Now back to our customer service manager who hates being bothered by customers. While this sounds ridiculous, we have all interacted with companies that give us the feeling that we are somehow bothering them by offering our business. Bear in mind, I am not talking about the inventor who thinks he has the next great product so he wastes the time of the manufacturer when in fact he has no marketing plan, no business plan, and no money to execute the product, the market, or himself. These folks truly are wasting the manufacturing firm's time.

Instead, I am talking about the firm that cannot see smoke for the fire beneath. There are so many instances where companies are doing just enough to break even while staving off the staggering success beating down their door.

Case in point, one of the firms that I ran had a division that produced custom-engineered mechanical components for several different industries. The components were sheet metal stamped parts, and they were used in everything from telecommunications equipment to medical devices, automotive parts to brackets for satellite dishes. It would not be unfair to state that a very large percentage of products that are used and sold in the U.S. have at least one sheet metal stamping in them or on them.

As you may have guessed, with such a large demand for this type of manufacturing there are quite a few manufacturers. However, there was and still is a wide spectrum of stampers with regard to quality, delivery, and pricing. In short, there are those that are very good and those that are very bad. The one I am referring to was one of those that was quite good.

During its formative years, opportunities were there for the picking. If you could make the part and could deliver sometime within a three-year window for a fair price, the job was yours. Of course, I am being facetious, but you get the idea.

Substantial market married with a capable supplier—what could possibly stop this company from flying high? The answer in a word: ownership. The owners had an odd approach to growth. They challenged their managers to take on additional capacity without adding additional equipment.

While this sounds like a good idea from the owner's standpoint, it had a serious flaw.

Every time additional work was brought through the factory, existing customers began to have their products shipped late. In order to make room for the new customers, the old customers would need to take a back seat. This made the customer list look like it was printed on a down escalator. Every time a new customer was added to the top of the list, an old customer would fall off the bottom of the list. Ten pounds of bologna in a five-pound bag. Something is going to squirt out somewhere. Sorry about the imagery.

The solution was painfully apparent to everyone, including ownership, or so I suspected. Buy additional equipment and then go out and get additional customers. Simple, right?

Not so fast. See, the problem ownership had was they were a very conservative sort. They did not believe in buying any equipment that did not have a customer waiting in the wings to buy its manufacturing time. In addition, ownership's understanding of modern capacity constraint loading was on par with manufacturing practices during the era of the Johnson administration. You remember this era. This was when the Japanese first started to beat the living crap out of U.S. manufacturing.

Combine a poor understanding of capacity management with a damaging approach to capacity constraints and what do you get? Well... growth for the first ten years. Not staggering growth but growth nonetheless. In the early years, ownership had to buy stamping presses without customer demand because the business was brand new. The rule that brought early success—buying equipment and then looking for business to fill the available capacity—was soon tossed out the door. In addition, the demand was so strong and the available supply chain was so weak that good things were going to happen irrespective of upper management.

Do you remember when the Dallas Cowboys' head coach Jimmy Johnson resigned and Barry Switzer took over? Barry won a Super Bowl with a team that Jimmy had groomed. Jerry Jones, the owner of the Cowboys, could have hired any of the cast from *Queer Eye for the Straight Guy* to manage the Cowboys and still produced a Super Bowl–winning team. And so went the success of this firm. Momentum from its earliest days forced success.

The environment was such that success was the norm instead of the exception from the mid 1980s through the mid 1990s. But then reality set in during the last of the Clinton years. The markets crashed not long after Janet Reno went after Microsoft, and the market-driven manufacturing environment began to fall apart.

It had been a very good run, however, for this manufacturer, going from zero sales to $10 million or so in gross revenues, soon to fall back to less than half of that in a twenty or so year period. Not bad... or was it?

Looking to other similar manufacturers whose dates closely mirrored those of the company I ran, we see similar growth with one exception. There was an additional zero behind all of their numbers. They had outperformed the company I had worked for by at least one order of magnitude. Do you remember what an order of magnitude is? Ten times the growth over the same period of time, in the same industry, and in many cases selling to the same customers. The manufacturer I was working for was doing quite well in spite of the ownership driving the boat. Or were they anchoring the boat?

I left the organization as I had determined that there was only so much I could learn working for folks who were only capable of teaching me what not to do. A few years later, after the company was continuing to waffle during more realistic economies following 9/11, the company was put on the block and sold. Sales numbers are, of course, private within a privately held company, but sources shared estimates of barely one times top-line revenue, which had faltered to the mid seven-figure mark—far below its height during the 1980s and less than one-tenth the value of a competitor that was recently sold.

Managing the dimes ad nauseam and not taking advantage of the "once in a lifetime" sales environment allowed the dollars to slip away. Please don't misunderstand me; the owners of this firm did quite well for themselves by most comparisons. After all, if you are given lemons and you make lemonade, you are to be commended. However, if you are given a goose that lays golden eggs and all you make is foie gras, you are to be caned about the head, neck, and shoulders.

IX. And the billboard read, "Entering the Middle..."

If you are foolish enough to get on the train to "nowhere," please don't be surprised when the conductor kicks you off at "anywhere." "No matter where you go, there you are." I could fill a paragraph or two with these.

Well, just a couple more from the great Yogi Berra: "I knew I was going to take the wrong train so I left early." And finally, "You've got to be very careful if you don't know where you're going, because you might not get there."

Many business owners start their businesses with the hope of becoming successful entrepreneurs. The problem with this is that *successful* is a very broad, sweeping term and extremely relative to the user. Many businesses that I have worked with either as a supplier to or a customer of are delusionally successful—they believe they can delude themselves into successfully surviving. Astonishingly enough, in many instances, they have been able to convince either a bank or an investment firm to share in their deluded state of mind.

The flip side of this coin is the stellar firm that is unaware of their potential and consequently undermines their own success with fears of victory. Their delusion is that they are afraid of being delusional. Almost circular logic, isn't it?

The one sure method for overcoming both of these extremes is to have a goal in mind. Being successful is like wishing someone a "good morning." It is generic and evokes a halfhearted response from both the well-wisher and the recipient. Neither really have any specifics in mind when these words are uttered. So much did this interchange intrigue me that I decided that for a period of one week, I would not greet anyone with the standard "good morning." Rather, I would grunt two bass notes, a kind of "ding-dong" in the lowest of tones that my closed mouth could produce.

Not only did not a single soul make eye contact with me, no one even glanced in my general direction. It's almost as if we are bees buzzing around a hive, and in order to keep civility, we occasionally throw each other a buzzing sound.

The funny thing is that we occasionally pay attention, and to this end, I will share the very last day of my grunting experiment. As I was leaving that fine

Friday afternoon, I passed the receptionist on the way out the door. I very clearly told her to "f— off." Of course, I apologized immediately and explained the experiment I was conducting. She accepted my apology and then proceeded to toss her cup of water at my crotch, her very cold cup of water.

So, I concluded that we are awake for the most part, but for some reason and in some circumstances, we are mesmerized or zombied into a state of catatonic grunts and groans. I have asked many small business owners for definitions of success, and few, if any, can give me a clearly defined answer. "Staying in business" and "Able to pay the bills" are not definitions of success. They are definitions of survival. No one I know wants to risk everything they have, which many small business owners have done and continue to do, just to survive.

Success is more than owning a job. It is more than just putting food on the table. It's putting very good food on the table and being able to remove oneself from the job if so desired.

I interviewed a small business owner recently and asked, "What do you feel you should have as a return for the personal risks that you have placed in your firm?" His response: "I am expecting $250K per year in income, taxable deductions to reduce that income to $85K, and a buyout in ten years of $5 to $7 million." That, my friends, is the difference between someone who owns a job and a true entrepreneur. To use baseball terminology, "now that's getting a little wood on the ball." Do you see the difference between this last answer and "Able to pay the bills"? The difference is not that of being fortunate or being lucky enough to make $250K. The difference is where attitude overcomes a lack of altitude. It's the owner propelling the firm rather than the firm anchoring its owner. This changes ownership from "in spite of" to "because of."

The difference between a business owner and one who merely owns a job is EXPECTATIONS. A true entrepreneur will quickly turn his nose up at a business model that requires him to spend all of his time "baking the pies." A true entrepreneur will find a way to automate or off-load the baking to a machine, hired labor, etc., in an effort to spend more time increasing sales, adding additional stores, selling online, etc. The job owner will complain that there just isn't enough time in the day.

I know you know what I'm talking about. We have all seen the business owner who is so mired down with the details of running the business, of "baking the pies," that we just know that this guy is going to fail in the end. At the very least, we think to ourselves, "Just sell the business and go to work for someone else. Your life will be so much better."

You know the type of person I am talking about. His desk is a disaster. He always looks unkempt and disheveled. He can't find anything he is looking for, and as he is looking, he stumbles across items that were opportunities to improve his business that are now six months old. You can hear him mumble under his breath, "I remember this; why didn't I take care of that? Oh well, too late now." But instead of throwing the item in the trash, it goes right back on the faded oak desk. Or at least you think it's oak; rumor has it it's oak.

I leave you with a famous quote from John Wayne: "Life's tough...It's even tougher if you're stupid." Overcome the lazy, stupid tendencies of being a business owner and have a plan—a written plan defining what success looks like. Or, as Yogi Berra said, "you might not get there."

X. Absence makes it look way too easy.

I wrestle with the following premise on a regular basis. The very best managers, owners, CEOs, etc. have one very odd resulting outcome in common. When they are gone, the sky doesn't fall, the walls don't come down, and the four horsemen don't begin their apocalyptic ride. When really good managers disappear, few even notice they're gone.

One of the best compliments I have ever heard someone utter regarding management skills was directed at my first superior, and it was not intended to be a compliment. My boss had, at that time, left the company he hired me to work for and had been gone for roughly five weeks. I was sorely missing him while he was on his way to the CEO's office at a Fortune 100 company.

A middle manager was recounting my boss's tenure at the company and uttered the most ridiculous statement that had passed between my then twenty-one-year-old ears. It went something like this: "If he was such a good manager, how is it he has been gone for more than a month now and we are still doing just as well as when he was here?" Even at twenty-one years of age, I recognized this as a foolish statement. This, of course, refers back to the whole Dallas Cowboys issue I brought up earlier. However, let me add something previously not brought up.

If you are paid to manage a company for someone else, you need to be careful you don't manage yourself right out of a job by proving how well things can run with or without you. If you are an entrepreneur, the task at hand is similar but with outcomes 180 degrees in the opposite direction. In theory, we are asked to create a company. Make it profitable. Make it viable. And then turn it over to let someone else run it into the ground. No wait, that's not right. I know a lot of business owners who can do that themselves and save themselves the manager's salary.

Of course, the true intent is to hand off the business to let someone else copy the business and then become your biggest competitor. Damn, I did it again. I know I can get this right. Let's start again. I know a lot of business owners who can leave the competitor issues to their brother-in-law.

The true intent is to hand off the business to someone who is properly motivated to run the business as if it were his own. In return, he successfully grows the business, having a stake in the business without having to take any of the entrepreneurial risks.

Just how is this accomplished? Well, there are dozens of ideas on this subject, but there are a few that I really like. First, take your time hiring and use all of the hiring tips in previous chapters. Second, perform all of the testing and background checks as suggested in previous chapters. Third, ask yourself and others, "What would make you motivated enough to run this business as if it were your baby?"

- A percentage of the company?
- A percentage of the net?
- Full ownership after five or ten years?
- Partial ownership after five or ten years?

There are many, many ideas that can be written, but don't fool yourself into believing that someone will have your best interest at heart for an extra $20K a year. If you want his heart, mind, and soul, then you're gonna have to pay for it. The reward?

Your company thrives and survives while you are busy starting your next enterprise, and the whole thing starts all over again. Or maybe you just sleep on a beach for a while. Your choice here.

Why not just keep running this business? Here is my theory of why this may not be the best idea:

There are people who are good at starting a business and taking it from $0 to $5 million.

There are people who are good at taking a business from $5 to $10 million.

There are people who are good at taking a business from $10 to $25 million.

There are people who are good at taking a business from $25 to $50 million.

There are people who are good at taking a business from $50 to $100 million and beyond.

Very rarely are these all the same person. Most entrepreneurs are in the $0 to $5 million category. Rarely do they break out to the next category and proceed upward. This is not an insult. Jack Welsh, former CEO of General Electric, alluded to the fact that his people were not smart enough to develop start-up businesses. Consequently, he was going to simply buy small businesses and grow them into large businesses. Jack Welsh is a pretty smart guy and did not hire idiots. If he felt this way, you can bet on the fact that starting a business is indeed difficult.

If your intent is to grow beyond $5 million, are you the most qualified to take your business that far? If growing beyond $5 million is not part of your mission, then you may want to skip ahead a bit.

The point is that each of these categories is run by individuals with specific talents and skill sets. Apple trees cannot grow oranges. Your job is to grow the best apples you can and leave it at that. Hopefully your skill set, as an entrepreneur, does not lie in the upper categories. If so, you're going to have an awful time establishing a $50 million business on day one.

Let me offer a perfect example to further illustrate why I believe in the categorization of skill sets among business owners. I am close friends with a couple that owns a business. In keeping their privacy, I am not going to share their industry but rather call their entity a bakery.

Their bakery is very successful for such a small community. In fact, it is so successful, it outperforms the nearest competitor by a two-to-one margin on gross sales as well as profits. No one can touch their numbers.

One evening, I asked what they attributed their success to, and I was told to ask another question—but with a smile. So I shifted in my chair and replied, "Let me rephrase that. Do you feel you have developed a marketing engine capable of duplicating itself?" I received an answer in the affirmative but still with a queried tone.

I quickly responded that I was not interested in entering into competition with my dear friends, but I was interested in exploring the possibility of creating a franchise out of their bakery model and pursuing this interest in distant cities. The reply I received from the wife of this couple left me quite stunned. "You can't do what we did in another city." I immediately inquired as to why.

"Other communities are vastly different than what we have here, and it just won't work." The wife of this couple is not by any means an ignorant person. On the contrary, she is quite shrewd and the main thrust behind their business, especially when you consider that the husband also works full time for another company. In effect, she has built the business from the fruits of her imagination. He has been there as support, a sounding board, and labor when needed.

So we must ask, what was in her thought process that would lead her to believe that our community was a vacuum in comparison to the remainder of the country? The easy answer is Texas is a place unlike any other. Just ask a Texan. My home state chauvinism aside, the correct answer is she doesn't believe we live in a vacuum. She does, however, believe that what she has been able to create is a bit of a hothouse orchid.

With very few exceptions, do any of our business entities exist in rarified air? Her brain was telling her that something indeed would be different in starting a duplicate business in another state. The response given showed that her belief that her business was nothing more than an anomaly was more than apparent. It was so very hard to believe that all of her hard work, all of the wonderful success she and her husband were experiencing, and the plight of those who counted themselves a competitor gave her little confidence in her abilities to "play it again, Sam."

She is, in fact and without a doubt, a $0 to $5 million entrepreneur. The mind-set of someone in the categories of $6 million and up would quickly jump to the conclusion that franchising this entity would be exceptionally viable.

Please do not misunderstand my critique; this is an extraordinary individual. Both she and her husband are outstanding folks. No one within a fifty-mile radius can even come close to their performance. They are the Boris Becker, Tiger Woods, Nolan Ryan, Larry Bird, and Joe Montana of the baking biz. They have developed a business that affords them a great deal of income and a great deal of time away from the office/oven. But they are not the Ray Crock of the cake world. And as I understand it, Ray Crock couldn't fry a burger to save his life.

Here lies my recommendation and frustration: take your skill set, develop your trade as an entrepreneur, and then let someone with the next skill set take it from there. Or not.

And this is where the rub lies and why I wrestle with this concept. I firmly believe in growing your business to its full potential, but what could be wrong with keeping your business at a level that is commensurate with your lifestyle demands? This I believe to be true especially if the business is not particularly demanding of your time and attention. I can't seem to argue with that statement. Can you? Maybe absence from your business just makes the heart grow fonder.

XI. Precision, Accuracy, and the difference between the two.

Before exiting this chapter, I would like to impart one last concept on you. The general public and especially the media use the two terms *precision* and *accuracy* almost interchangeably. Nothing can be further from the truth, and these two terms are critical to the success of any business.

Some organizations have high degrees of precision but poor accuracy. Others are fairly accurate but lack precision. So let me define these terms as used in science, engineering, statistics, and industry.

Precision is repeatability. Using a dartboard analogy, if you were a very precise dart thrower, all of your darts would be very close to each other. The distance from dart to dart would be less than a quarter of an inch. This, however, does not address the fact that all of your darts are stuck in the pinball machine next to the dartboard...but they are very close together.

Accuracy is nearness to target. If the target is the bull's eye in the center of the dartboard and you are an accurate dart thrower, all of your darts will be in and around the bull's eye, but they may not be close to each other. Your darts may be above the bull's eye, beneath the bull's eye, or to one side or the other but with very little repeatability. The measurement between darts may be as high as five or six inches.

If your business is run with great precision, you will notice that you consistently show similar results regardless of the circumstances that surround your business. Great effort will be necessary in making even the slightest improvements to your organization. Conversely, enormous effort will be required to damage your organization. In effect, companies that run with great precision are the proverbial unstoppable force. Little can stop you. Marvelous characteristics as long as you're not going off a cliff.

If your business is run with great accuracy, you have strong tendencies to fulfill your goals but do so with a lot of course corrections, not to mention a lot of smoke-and-mirror-type efforts. Little can annoy you. Marvelous characteristics as long as you constantly work the rudder.

Taking note of your organization's repeatability (precision) and nearness to your targets (accuracy) will help you make decisions as to whether any risk is worth its reward. For instance, if your organization is constantly making the same mistake over and over, and the desire is to make a change to remove the mistake, but your folks are performing extremely well in all other aspects, you may choose to live with the mistake on a repetitive basis. Pulling the one weed in the garden may sound like a good idea until its root splits and creates two dozen new weeds.

I refer to Bill Cosby, who asked a cocaine user what made that drug so wonderful. The cocaine user responded that use of cocaine intensified his personality. Bill quickly retorted, "Well, yes, but what if you're an asshole?"

Having a highly precise company is great if you're near the target. Consistently doing the same thing day in and day out is extremely beneficial if your results are desirable but can be devastating if the results are detrimental.

Having a highly accurate company is great as long as you under-promise and over-deliver. High accuracy usually necessitates a lot of target practice and demanding requirements of your people. In turn, they become better skilled at a wider array of tasks, where a precision company relies more on standardization than intuition.

Combining the two produces a wicked combination of capabilities woven in a fabric of skill sets that can propel an organization into the kind of growth that will often set the owner's hair on fire—wonderful to watch and painful to compete against.

Chapter 6

Margins, Spirals, and Screws, Oh My!

Deregulation of energy companies is no longer a topic of conversation in Texas as this happened many years ago. Many other states deregulated their power companies as well. Deregulation lowered the water line, revealing a rather interesting concept in the energy sector. Power companies must maintain and operate a minimum amount of electrical capacity. This capacity must be equal to or greater than the maximum amount of electrical consumption for the previous year or years. Different states do the calculations differently, but by and large, the target is that each power supplier must maintain and operate as a very minimum the capacity to cover the very largest amount of electricity demand they will ever see. For some of the larger metropolitan areas, this could mean dozens of power plants, even if there are several power companies supplying to the same area. Prior to deregulation, this was a requirement, but with states issuing the value placed on a kilowatt-hour of electricity, it was never really an issue.

Obviously, some of the plants are not running at full capacity all of the time. Months when air temperatures are more moderate will likely demand less electrical supply than the months when air conditioners or heaters are running full tilt. However, the power companies must have the requirements for July and August as well as January and February covered with the capability of supplying whatever demands we can throw at them. Since power plants cannot be turned on like a light switch, these plants need to be supplying high levels of electricity even if there are no customers to accept the supplied power, especially during the above-mentioned four months.

So I have a question for you. If you are a power supplier, and we are sitting in the middle of August, and suddenly 5 percent of your customers leave, for whatever reason, what do you do?

As a power supplier, you can maybe turn off a turbine or two, but you still have several dozen power plants to keep running. Turning off a turbine will save some of your overhead but not nearly enough to compensate for the loss, and you still run the risk of the summer heat setting a record high and demand exceeding supply at a time when you just turned off a turbine. Not a wise thing to do unless you live in Southern California.

The obvious answer is to raise the price of electricity. As a response to the price increase, you lose another 5 percent of your customer base. You shut down another turbine, but this does not cover the additional lost revenue, so you raise prices again. And again, you lose another 5 percent of your customer base.

In theory, you can get to where you have only one customer paying for the entire overhead of a power company. Obviously, this will not happen, but you can see where the power company can get itself into real trouble by losing too many customers. The folks in the power industry call this a death spiral. Why should you care about an energy sector death spiral?

I'm telling you this story in order to illustrate a specific point concerning your margins. When calculating what you believe your profits before taxes will be, you should be very careful to analyze these figures in two ways. One way is where the death spiral is pulling your company skyward like a tornado, and everything is peaches and cream. You are growing, and your biggest concern is how you are going to expand to handle the growth. Obviously a death spiral that continues to grow and grow your customers beyond your capability to service these customers can crush your organization. Don't believe me? Ask a "retired" exec with AOL.

The other way to run these numbers is where the death spiral is pulling your company downward like the flushing of a toilet—apt analogy, eh? Your concerns here are that you are losing customers and you are trying to maintain your margins on fewer and fewer customers.

The main question to ask yourself is, how scaleable is your organization? This is a fancy way of asking the following simple question. If I have only 75 percent of the business I think I am going to have, can I operate with only 75 percent of the overhead I think I am going to have? If my customers are 50 percent of my target business level, can I operate with 50 percent of my target overhead? I am referring to this as a linear business. Academics have a lot of different ways of describing this, but linear is a simple way. If you are linear in the nature of your business model, you have a distinct advantage over many of the organizations out there.

It is understood that the marketplace determines what someone will pay for goods or services. The best pricing analogy I can offer is the turning of a screw. Like tightening a screw, your customers should provide a little resistance to your pricing. Overt resistance means your pricing is in the outer orbits of the planet somewhere and unsustainable in the marketplace. Conversely, immediate pricing acceptance from a customer means you are leaving money on the table.

Laughter through tears is described by many as a favorite emotion. When it comes to setting your pricing, you are looking for eventual acceptance through temperate shock.

What drives your margins and how you develop your margins are controlled by one person: you. If you cannot make the numbers work for what you feel is a minimally acceptable margin, you need to walk away from that particular business model and find one that does work. Remember, it must work during a death spiral. In other words, it must work during the lean times where you have lost 50 percent of your top-line business. If it doesn't, you are risking losing your business or, at the very least, owning a job.

I recently spoke to the wife of a business owner who completed a bankruptcy on his organization, and unfortunately, it will not emerge. The entire business is a loss. I, of course, asked what happened.

She explained that he had been working sixty plus hours a week trying to make ends meet, pulling resources from banks, individuals, investment firms, etc. in an all-out effort to hold the company together. I asked how long he had been in that 911 mode. She said for the last two years.

"The last two years?!?" I exclaimed. She said with great pride that he was so determined to save his company that he would have done anything to make it work. I replied by first offering my most heartfelt condolences on the loss of the business. Second, I assured her that my questions were of mere interest and were not intended to have her relive this epic adventure and asked her to please excuse me if I strike a nerve. She understood.

"Wouldn't it have been better if he was hit by a bus?" I asked. "Two years of struggling with the eventual death of a business is more than anyone should be asked to endure."

I could tell she was taken aback by my question, and she sheepishly added that at the time it looked like the business would have made it out of bankruptcy. "At what time? During the first three months? The first six months? The first year? The second year?" Yes, of course, companies have been in and out of bankruptcy over a two-year period and have survived. (All two of them.) But to hang on to an organization that is obviously defunct and pour that kind of time and energy into it will take the wind out of the sails of anyone.

I continued, "Wouldn't it have been better to end the business after five or six months when the ink from the writing on the wall was still moist? And then apply that energy to a new entity, one with a chance for survival?"

Her response was that all along "he felt the company would eventually survive. After all, the business had been profitable for two whole years."

"Two whole years?!?" I rebuked. "Two years is nowhere near enough to judge whether a business is viable. That's like basing your sexual prowess on a one-night stand. The jury is still out."

"When you said the margins were good, what did you mean?" I asked.

"Well, I'm not really sure, but I remember breaking even the second year," she said. At this point, my brain was ready to explode.

"You only broke even, and you consider this a good year? Please have your husband call me before he starts a new business. I may be able to help him."

Let me share with you my thoughts on margins. Obviously, the above example was not something I would describe as a success story. The intent of the story is not the horrible financial results but rather the death grip that the owner placed on the organization. The company had failed. Bury the dead. Words of wisdom from one of my favorite poets, A. E. Housman:

"The cow, the old cow, she is dead; It sleeps well, the horned head: We poor lads, 'tis our turn now."

Stock traders will tell you to never fall in love with a stock. I am telling you to never fall in love with your company. You may spend more time with her than you do with your spouse, but she is not a member of the family. Your business is more like a car. When the cost of maintenance no longer makes sense, it's time to let her go.

Cars begin to fail you with breakdowns. Businesses will fail you with poor returns. If the CDs from the neighborhood bank can outperform your business, it's time to bury the cow. As a matter of fact, I would expect at least 10 percent profit from your business as a bare minimum after you pay yourself but before taxes. Anything less than this, unless unusually low efforts are required to run the entity, and you will be doing yourself a great injustice.

Chapter 7

There's No Place Like Home

I was born in the Northeast. I was raised in the Northeast, and I was educated in the Northeast. It was a wonderful place to grow up, and until I started making moves (mostly south and west), I did not realize other places in this country were wonderful as well.

Don't misunderstand me; I truly love many things about each and every place that I have lived. Some have great sports; some have great food; some have better traffic; and almost all have good people. But few have acceptable costs of living. Let's call a spade a spade. If you can't afford to live the lifestyle you deserve because the cost of living in your state is too high, what's the point? I guess you can wave at your favorite restaurants as you drive by them, not being able to afford their menus. I suppose you can sigh as you pass the neighborhoods in which you can't afford to buy even the smallest of homes.

Wealth accumulation for most folks is hindered by several factors, such as mortgages, credit cards, etc. But for business owners, the largest threat to wealth accumulation is taxes. And for us, the main reason why we can't live in our neighborhood of choice or dine regularly at the restaurant of our choosing is taxes. Don't believe me?

Re-run all of your financials without paying a dime in taxes and see what your new net income becomes. I don't know you. I don't know your business. But I am reasonably confident that your new net income, without taxes, has launched like a Trident missile. Beware of all of the space junk.

We all have places of choice where we wish to live. I would suggest reading the following article by Arthur Laffer and Stephen Moore before you make any final decisions. It is titled "Soak the Rich, Lose the Rich," dated May 2009. And before your skepticism becomes inflamed at making a decision on the location of your business based solely on one article, there are dozens of similar articles with hundreds of facts and figures to back up this information. You may turn these pages and succumb to a differing opinion, but you may not detract from their facts.

For simplicity, I am going to hit only the highlights of the article. Laffer and Moore write:

> Lawmakers in California, Connecticut, Delaware, Illinois, Minnesota, New Jersey, New York and Oregon want to raise income tax rates on the top 1% or 2% or 5% of their citizens. New Illinois Gov. Patrick Quinn wants a 50% increase on the income tax rate on the wealthy because this is the 'fair' way to close his state's gaping deficit.
>
> Here's the problem for states that want to pry more money out of the wallets of rich people. It never works because people,

investment capital, and businesses are mobile: they can leave tax-unfriendly states and move to tax-friendly states. The tax differential between low-tax states is widening, meaning that relocation from high-tax California or Ohio, to no-income tax Texas or Tennessee, is all the more financially profitable both in terms of lower tax bills and more job opportunities. Updating some research from Richard Vedder of Ohio University, we found that from 1998 to 2007, more than 1100 people every day including Sundays and holidays moved from the nine highest income-tax states such as California, New Jersey, New York, and Ohio and relocated mostly to the nine tax-haven states with no income tax, including Florida, Nevada, New Hampshire, and Texas. We also found that over these same years the no-income tax states created 89% more jobs and had 32% faster personal income growth than their high-tax counterparts.

Are you starting to see the light yet? Continuing with the article:

> Did the greater prosperity in low-tax states happen by chance? Is it coincidence that the two highest tax-rate states in the nation, California and New York, have the biggest fiscal holes to repair? No. Dozens of academic studies – old and new – have found clear and irrefutable statistical evidence that high state and local taxes repel jobs and businesses.

Where is your business located again? Are you sure you want to stay there? If you're thinking that most people are born, live, and die in the same city or state, your thinking is flat wrong. States that have increased taxes on their richest taxpayers have seen significant reductions in numbers of people paying taxes in these brackets even when compared to the national average. And yes, this comparison was completed during our nation's strongest economic times, 2004 to 2006. During this time, the stock market was booming and Wall Street earnings exceeded trillions of dollars. Studies have shown that these folks either moved or simply stopped paying their tax bills. In either case, the states that have raised tax rates, in the end, are the biggest losers.

Remember, the notion that millionaires won't move is ridiculous. These folks are extremely mobile, as are their investments. Many of the high-tax states' richest folks sell their homes and leave. The rich who choose to stay behind begin to report lower incomes in order to combat the higher tax bills. What is even more difficult to measure are the vast numbers of folks who will not even consider moving to these states because of the income tax structures the state governments offer. As stated earlier, "89% of incomes over $50,000 a year are earned by owners of small businesses." How many jobs are lost each year by states because the business owners who would be bringing these jobs refuse to move to those states because of the tax rates? Could this be why high income-tax states have such difficulties creating job growth?

The argument for lower taxes is generally combated from the other side with statements that lowering tax rates results in states competing for the bottom or the Wal-Mart approach to attracting companies to their state. This could not be further from the truth.

I return to our article:

> They're wrong, and New Hampshire is our favorite illustration. The Live Free or Die State has no income or sales tax, yet it has high-quality schools and excellent public services. Students in New Hampshire public schools achieve the fourth-highest test scores in the nation – even though the state spends about $1,000 a year less per resident on state and local government than the average state and, incredibly, $5,000 less per person than New York. And on the other side of the ledger, California in 2007 had the highest-paid classroom teachers in the nation, and yet the Golden State had the second-lowest test scores.

To drive this point home, I would contrast New Jersey and Texas. New Jersey has one of the highest income tax structures in the country, and its sales taxes are exceptionally high as well, and yet it is consistently running deficits with some of the worst schools in the nation. Texas, on the other hand, has no state income tax and actually cut taxes in 2009. In 2008, Texas created more jobs than all other states combined. Can you guess where business owners were moving to during 2008? Texas is a great state, but its government did not create all of those jobs. Most were brought to the state by business owners looking to relocate their businesses in a tax-friendly environment.

Texas has its fair share of problems—I freely admit this—but do you really need me to explain why I have placed my business in Texas?

Ultimately, the decision in selecting a state in which to place your business is yours and yours alone. There may be factors such as proximity to family, proximity to friends, etc. that may influence your decision, but I must remind you that these are influencing factors. They are not decision makers.

Decision makers are things such as proximity to customers, proximity to vendors, proximity to a capable workforce (this one can be arguable in any state), cost of living, and so on.

Chapter 8

One Ball – Two Eyes

[The following story comes via a close friend and colleague of mine. His background mimicked mine in many ways, and we quickly became very close friends. He and I have shared many stories over the years. I asked him to relay this story in the first person, as he shared it with me.]

The scene was the cafeteria of our facility. The year was 1996, and I was the general manager of Manufacturer XYZ in North Texas. The audience was the plant's full complement of employees: hourly, salary, temps, ownership, etc. They even brought back some folks who used to work there. If you have ever walked down our street, I think you would have been invited. Get the picture? The meeting was mandatory. The topic was our quality control systems, or so my upper management thought.

For months I had been browbeaten over quality mistakes and the resulting fallout of customers. The fact that the facility had been making more gross income and vastly improved sales seemed irrelevant.

The problem I had discovered was that there were a half-dozen or so clients that were draining 80 percent plus of our resources, and none of them were profitable for our facility. Our outside sales reps were making a killing on their sales, and unfortunately, the reps had the ears of ownership, who coincidentally came up the ranks through outside sales and only by a twist of fate became owners. So you can appreciate the fact that these six customers were the diametric opposites of redheaded stepchildren. They were to be protected at all costs by the walls of towers and the moats of the owners' castle.

The day's speech was intended by ownership to be a battle cry to improve our customer service and pricing to six target customers whose sole capability was to put us out of business, if we were lucky. The battleground of protection had been laid with catapults, trebuchets, and English longbows. Unfortunately, their field captain (namely me) showed up with an Abram's tank packing an AK-47 and quickly turned on his own side. I felt like Chuck Norris, Arnold Schwarzenegger, and Sylvester Stallone all rolled into one that day. I truly was a one-man wrecking crew. The carnage began with one question: "What is the most important thing we do here?"

The cafeteria grew painfully silent. The seconds that ensued ticked by like hours. No one dared to speak in fear of being incorrect, or in fear of being correct, or in fear of displaying any signs of breathing. The crew had been beaten into submission by ownership when independent thought had shown signs of life in the past, and they were not going to make that mistake again. Fortunately, I was prepared for such a contingency.

Sue Ellen Michaels, the nineteen-year-old new girl, was too new to remember past cafeteria meetings and too young to realize her role as a pawn. I, looking directly at her, fed her the line that would launch her answer to my question, and right on cue, there it was: "The most important thing we do here is make money." The whole of the room took a short but unmistakable gasp. I could feel ownerships' eyes upon me as daggers began to fly across the black-and-white checkerboard vinyl-clad tiled flooring. The chess game was on.

Quickly I showed support for Sue Ellen's reply to my question of why we all worked at that facility. "To make money!" I exclaimed at the top of my lungs. "To prove this simple theory, let me ask a few very simple questions," I added.

"If we have the very best products on the face of the planet but still fail to make money, will we survive?" The low murmur from the audience was barely audible but unmistakable and answered in the negative. I continued, "If we have the very best customer service and force all of our competitors out of business so we are the only supplier left but still fail to make money, will we survive?" Again, the answer was faint but still answered in the negative. "If we have the most expensive or the least expensive products, will it matter if we don't make any money?" Now beginning to gain some volume, the crowd responded in the negative to my question.

Starting to feel like some sort of industrial tent revival preacher, I began to walk back and forth across the chessboard, my pace matching the rhythm of my speech pattern.

"So regardless of how good or bad of a company we are, nothing really matters if we don't make money. Are you with me?" God help me, but some of the folks were now beginning to clap in agreement, and I was really enjoying myself. I only wish I had an 800 number for the folks at home to call in—just kidding. Back to the sermon, or rather, back to the meeting.

I then asked, "If making money is the most important thing we can do here, what is the biggest risk to our organization?" Now shouting at the top of their voices, many were heard to say, "Anything that keeps us from making money." Halleluiah, I had gotten through to these people. And I had also angered ownership beyond human comprehension. Oh yeah, I was going to get fired that day anyway, so I decided to go out with a bang.

"You all have worked here for quite a while." (All except Sue Ellen, and she was about to beat me out the door.) "You all know what causes this organization to lose money. You all know this better than I." And God as my witness, I cannot lie, almost to a person they began to rattle off the list of clients that I knew we needed to get rid of and send to our competitors. I knew the list, and now they knew the list. And ownership knew I knew. And all of the employees knew I knew, and they knew that ownership knew they knew. And then I slowly walked over to Sue Ellen, looked deeply into her dark blue eyes, and whispered, "Checkmate."

Later, I helped Sue Ellen with her last box of personal effects as we both were escorted out of the building. No, I'm not kidding. This stunt cost me my job as well as Sue Ellen's. The upshot was I took her with me to my next job...working for the competition. You see, word traveled fast in our little industry, and the owner of a major competitor heard about my fanatical speech and offered me the GM position on the spot. He agreed with me and my thoughts of what makes a company great. Within a year, we had doubled our sales and were well on our way to dominating the industry. XYZ was spiraling out of control and was now less than half of their size when I left. Luckily for me, and the balance of our competitors, XYZ still had all six pitiful clients and had vowed to stay by their side into the abyss. Happy travels.

[The point of this story is that there is only one point to being in business, and the owners of XYZ had lost sight of this. We don't do what we do because we think we need the practice. We all love to have happy customers, but this is not the point. We all love to improve the lives of the people and the companies that do business with us, but this is not the point. Making inroads into lifting the human condition is a wonderful endeavor, but this is not the point. Make no mistake; if you are in business, you are there to turn a profit. The balance is wonderful cocktail rhetoric but little else. Being in business and not making money is like holding a global warming meeting during a record blizzard. It might make you "feel," but it won't make you "result."]

Epilogue

In the end, I believe in three elements to a successfully run business. First, select your business model carefully. Not only must all of the numbers work, but you must also have all of the necessary "ins" and "outs" of success. "Ins" would be all of the inputs to your business. This is the feeding of your business and includes items such as labor, vendors, location, and the like. "Outs" are the means to the ends. This would include your customers, performance targets, margins, and wealth accumulation to eventually remove the necessity of your presence in day-to-day operations.

Second, I feel very strongly that it is more important to pay the bills than it is to have a feeling of fulfillment from your firm. Fulfillment comes from family, faith, and friends. While a burning passion for your business may help push you through tough times, it may also cloud your judgment and keep you in a business model that in the end eventually fails. While waking up in the morning and being eager to get to work may sound great (and I have been there), leave the love for a job to your employees. Entrepreneurs must be objective and far less emotional. Remember, never fall in love with a stock, and never ever fall in love with your business.

Last, I wish you passion. Not to contradict the former paragraph, I am not speaking of passion for your firm. I am wishing you passion to push through the pains of the start-up organization. Push through the customers that will never give you even the slightest chance. Push through the competitors that are ruining otherwise great margins. Push through the governmental regulations, government fees, and taxes in general. Push through the class envy and class warfare the media will pound endlessly. I wish you the passion to follow what you feel you can do. Amaze yourself.

Some days you will feel that you can't go on. Some days you will feel that nothing can stop you. In business, the call is yours, and you will probably be right regardless of what day it is.

www.ingramcontent.com/pod-product-compliance
Lightning Source LLC
Chambersburg PA
CBHW051530170526
45165CB00002B/681